T0123684

MACAT

An Analysis of

Theda Skocpol's

States and Social Revolutions:

A Comparative Analysis of France, Russia, and China

Riley Quinn

Published by Macat International Ltd
24:13 Coda Centre, 189 Munster Road, London SW6 6AW.

Distributed exclusively by Routledge
2 Park Square, Milton Park, Abingdon, Oxon OX14 4RN
711 Third Avenue, New York, NY 10017, USA

Routledge is an imprint of the Taylor & Francis Group, an informa business

www.macat.com
info@macat.com

Cataloguing in Publication Data
A catalogue record for this book is available from the British Library.
Library of Congress Cataloguing-in-Publication Data is available upon request.
Cover illustration: Etienne Gilfillan

ISBN 978-1-912303-46-5 (hardback)
ISBN 978-1-912128-49-5 (paperback)
ISBN 978-1-912282-34-0 (e-book)

Notice
The information in this book is designed to orientate readers of the work under analysis,
to elucidate and contextualise its key ideas and themes, and to aid in the development
of critical thinking skills. It is not meant to be used, nor should it be used, as a
substitute for original thinking or in place of original writing or research. References and
notes are provided for informational purposes and their presence does not constitute
endorsement of the information or opinions therein. This book is presented solely for
educational purposes. It is sold on the understanding that the publisher is not engaged
to provide any scholarly advice. The publisher has made every effort to ensure that
this book is accurate and up-to-date, but makes no warranties or representations with
regard to the completeness or reliability of the information it contains. The information
and the opinions provided herein are not guaranteed or warranted to produce particular
results and may not be suitable for students of every ability. The publisher shall not be
liable for any loss, damage or disruption arising from any errors or omissions, or from
the use of this book, including, but not limited to, special, incidental, consequential or
other damages caused, or alleged to have been caused, directly or indirectly, by the
information contained within.

CONTENTS

THE MACAT LIBRARY

The Macat Library is a series of unique academic explorations of seminal works in the humanities and social sciences – books and papers that have had a significant and widely recognised impact on their disciplines. It has been created to serve as much more than just a summary of what lies between the covers of a great book. It illuminates and explores the influences on, ideas of, and impact of that book. Our goal is to offer a learning resource that encourages critical thinking and fosters a better, deeper understanding of important ideas.

Each publication is divided into three Sections: Influences, Ideas, and Impact. Each Section has four Modules. These explore every important facet of the work, and the responses to it.

This Section-Module structure makes a Macat Library book easy to use, but it has another important feature. Because each Macat book is written to the same format, it is possible (and encouraged!) to cross-reference multiple Macat books along the same lines of inquiry or research. This allows the reader to open up interesting interdisciplinary pathways.

To further aid your reading, lists of glossary terms and people mentioned are included at the end of this book (these are indicated by an asterisk [*] throughout) – as well as a list of works cited.

Macat has worked with the University of Cambridge to identify the elements of critical thinking and understand the ways in which six different skills combine to enable effective thinking.
Three allow us to fully understand a problem; three more give us the tools to solve it. Together, these six skills make up the **PACIER** model of critical thinking. They are:

ANALYSIS – understanding how an argument is built
EVALUATION – exploring the strengths and weaknesses of an argument
INTERPRETATION – understanding issues of meaning

CREATIVE THINKING – coming up with new ideas and fresh connections
PROBLEM-SOLVING – producing strong solutions
REASONING – creating strong arguments

To find out more, visit **WWW.MACAT.COM.**

CRITICAL THINKING AND *STATES AND SOCIAL REVOLUTIONS*

Primary critical thinking skill: PROBLEM-SOLVING
Secondary critical thinking skill: INTERPRETATION

Many people want to understand what revolutions are and – especially – how they come about, from the academics who study them to the states that wish to prevent (or, in some cases, provoke) them. But it is arguably the US scholar Theda Skocpol who has done most to create a viable model of revolution, and *States and Social Revolutions* is the work in which she sets out her intellectual stall.

Skocpol's magnum opus can be considered a classic product of the critical thinking skill of problem-solving. She assesses several different revolutions – those of France, Russia and China – and asks new, productive questions about their causes and outcomes. The answers, collectively, allow her to move beyond existing theories such as the 'voluntarist' school (which suggests that revolutionaries have agency) and the Marxist school (which sees state institutions as nothing more than a front for class interests).

Skocpol's model assumes that states are autonomous bureaucratic institutions, which act in their own interests – a fundamental re-imagining based on fresh interpretations of the evidence. Her analysis extends beyond the causes of revolution to their consequences, and her argument that the revolutionary state that survives is the one that successfully implements a far-reaching program of reform helps to explain not only why the three revolutions she studied have proved enduringly influential, but also why hundreds of others, less successful, are barely remembered today.

ABOUT THE AUTHOR OF THE ORIGINAL WORK

Born in 1949 in the American Midwest, **Theda Skocpol** emerged in the late 1970s as one of the most challenging and original thinkers in the discipline of sociology. Her doctoral studies at Harvard led her to the conclusion that something akin to a scientific approach could be used to explain events as complex and perplexing as the French, Russian, and Chinese revolutions. Skocpol's later work broadened her area of study, and she particularly focused on the development of welfare states, but her contribution to thinking about revolutions is still considered extremely important.

ABOUT THE AUTHOR OF THE ANALYSIS

Riley Quinn holds master's degrees in politics and international relations from both LSE and the University of Oxford.

ABOUT MACAT

GREAT WORKS FOR CRITICAL THINKING

Macat is focused on making the ideas of the world's great thinkers accessible and comprehensible to everybody, everywhere, in ways that promote the development of enhanced critical thinking skills.

It works with leading academics from the world's top universities to produce new analyses that focus on the ideas and the impact of the most influential works ever written across a wide variety of academic disciplines. Each of the works that sit at the heart of its growing library is an enduring example of great thinking. But by setting them in context – and looking at the influences that shaped their authors, as well as the responses they provoked – Macat encourages readers to look at these classics and game-changers with fresh eyes. Readers learn to think, engage and challenge their ideas, rather than simply accepting them.

'Macat offers an amazing first-of-its-kind tool for interdisciplinary learning and research. Its focus on works that transformed their disciplines and its rigorous approach, drawing on the world's leading experts and educational institutions, opens up a world-class education to anyone.'

Andreas Schleicher
Director for Education and Skills, Organisation for Economic Co-operation and Development

'Macat is taking on some of the major challenges in university education … They have drawn together a strong team of active academics who are producing teaching materials that are novel in the breadth of their approach.'

Prof Lord Broers,
former Vice-Chancellor of the University of Cambridge

'The Macat vision is exceptionally exciting. It focuses upon new modes of learning which analyse and explain seminal texts which have profoundly influenced world thinking and so social and economic development. It promotes the kind of critical thinking which is essential for any society and economy. This is the learning of the future.'

Rt Hon Charles Clarke, former UK Secretary of State for Education

'The Macat analyses provide immediate access to the critical conversation surrounding the books that have shaped their respective discipline, which will make them an invaluable resource to all of those, students and teachers, working in the field.'

Professor William Tronzo, University of California at San Diego

WAYS IN TO THE TEXT

KEY POINTS

- Born in 1947, Theda Skocpol is an American sociologist,* who remains among the most prominent in the discipline. Sociology is the study of the history and functioning of human society.

- In her 1979 book *States and Social Revolutions: A Comparative Analysis of France, Russia, and China*, Skocpol argues that revolutions occur when a number of factors combine to disrupt state power, creating certain necessary conditions.

- Because revolutions are still a part of the world's political landscape today, what typically happens in any given revolution has important lessons.

Who Is Theda Skocpol?

Theda Skocpol, the author of *States and Social Revolutions: A Comparative Analysis of France, Russia, and China* (1979), is a renowned scholar of sociology at Harvard University in the United States. Born in 1947, she is most famous for her theory of revolution; she has also made significant contributions in other areas, including the development of welfare states* (systems in which a nation's government ensures the good health and economic well-being of the least prosperous). This is mainly achieved through things such as pensions and benefits (grants), and tends to focus on those in the greatest need.

Skocpol's parents were both teachers, and inspired her to become a scholar.[1] She began her academic career at Michigan State University in sociology and graduated, top of her class, in 1969. Her impressive grades won her a scholarship to pursue graduate work at Harvard.

At Harvard, Skocpol's association with prominent sociologists, including the political scholars Seymour Martin Lipset* and Barrington Moore,* shaped her thinking, with Moore perhaps the most influential. Skocpol took his graduate seminar for two consecutive years. Instead of engaging with theory, Moore had his students actually *do* historical sociology: they formulated their own answers to problems rather than simply studying the answers of others. Skocpol herself said that without this seminar she might not have come to look at the theories behind revolutions at all because there were so many competing explanations already.[2]

Skocpol won the prestigious Johan Skytte Prize in Political Science in 2007, and has served as president of the American Political Science Association* and as dean of graduate studies at Harvard.

What Does *States and Social Revolutions* Say?

In *States and Social Revolutions*, Skocpol begins by defining a social revolution* as a rapid, total change in all elements of society. This includes the political institutions *and* the basis of social relations. For example, the French Revolution,* which began in 1789, altered the form of government from a monarchy* (hereditary rule by a royal) to a republic* (democratic rule by citizens). It also reduced the privileges of the aristocracy* (the hereditary elite) and the Church, while instituting an entirely new social order famously based on "liberty, equality, and brotherhood."

Skocpol is interested in what makes social revolutions occur. At the time she wrote *States and Social Revolutions* in 1979, theories emphasized the role of individuals. People would revolt, it was argued, feeling themselves deprived of what they believe they *should* have, or because they transfer their loyalty to an authority other than the existing government, or because social values (equality, for example) and the rulers in government (the aristocracy, for example) cannot be reconciled. The social analysis of Marxist* theory has offered an influential explanation for the occurrence of revolutions; according to Marxist thought, every society creates winners and losers, and the losers inevitably mobilize and seize freedom for themselves: revolutions are the inevitable product of historical change.

Skocpol found these theories wanting. For example, "voluntarist" theories (that is, where people revolt because they *decide* to) are unable to account for why peasants around the world, all of whom have excellent reasons to revolt because they are excluded from most of the benefits of society, often do not revolt. Why did dispossessed French peasants revolt in the eighteenth century, while Russian peasants waited until the twentieth century? They were equally downtrodden, in some senses more so. Skocpol is also unconvinced by the Marxist idea that state institutions are nothing but puppet institutions of the dominant classes. Her own concept of the state is that it is a bureaucratic organization with its own interests, free to act autonomously (that is, independently of elites).

In her work, Skocpol argues that France, Russia, and China were all similar in important ways. All three were agrarian* autocracies* (that is, they were societies based on agricultural economies, ruled by a single person). They all faced a military threat from abroad that compelled them to modernize* rapidly, and this pressure created a rift between ruling elites and local landowning elites. Elites, by virtue of their birth, had been able to enjoy privileged status; the habit of "buying" a good position in either government or the military clearly showed that it was not always the most competent people holding these important positions, and the modernization process brought this to light.

Removing these privileges, and provoking resentment amongst people of high social status, generally creates the right conditions for revolution. In sociological terms, structure—already fragile states facing a variety of external threats—brings about revolutionary situations.

The prerevolutionary social order and the constraints states experience from things such as the resistance of elites, pressure from abroad, the necessity of economic development, and so on, determine the form of the postrevolutionary state. In all three cases that Skocpol investigated, revolutions resulted in powerful, centralized states because a new system of rule tends to drive quickly towards bureaucratization,* with government needing large numbers of technical experts acting in an administrative capacity. A new revolutionary system also moves towards rationalization:* changes in the way things are done so as to make them more efficient and predictable. Skocpol argues that the more reform a newly-revolutionary state needs, the more institutionally strong that state will become. France had a state institution that did not depend exclusively on the government, and became more democratic. China and Russia became much more centralized and bureaucratically powerful.

Why Does *States and Social Revolutions* Matter?
In the period just after *States and Social Revolutions* appeared, the world saw a wave of revolutionary change. Iran, Nicaragua and much of Latin America, and then postcommunist* Eastern Europe all experienced revolutions. In recent times, meanwhile, we have seen uprisings throughout the Arab world and continued unrest that casts doubt on what future states will look like.

States and Social Revolutions matters because it was one of the first works to provide important alternative explanations of revolution in place of that proposed by Marxism. It can still help us make sense of revolutionary change today. It is not that there were no alternative theories, but Marxism was the most widely accepted explanation of what revolution was, and why revolutions happened.

If *States and Social Revolutions* examined revolutions in ways that were more actively scientific than alternative explanations, it is because Skocpol employed a large quantity of data to help her make more empirical deductions* about the causes of revolutions (that is, deductions based on evidence verifiable by observation), rather than coming to conclusions through abstract theorizing about psychology or history.

States and Social Revolutions has inspired much subsequent inquiry in fields such as the relationship between international forces, domestic institutions, and the effect of both on shaping the future of states. Scholars such as the sociologists Jeff Goodwin,* Timothy Wickham-Crowley,* and Jack Goldstone* have continued to use Skocpol's method and focus, and have applied them to the twentieth and twenty-first centuries. Skocpol wrote about modernizing revolutions arising from the tension created as societies based on farming undergo the transformation to societies based on industry. Revolutions today, however, look different. Urbanization, technological advances, religious ideology, the possibility of joining a democratic international order: all these have fundamentally changed what theorists examine when trying to understand what sparks a revolution. The international relations* theorist George Lawson,* for example, sees revolutionary change as coming about through "negotiation" rather than violence, because revolutionaries are looking for liberty within an already existing democratic international order, rather than some sort of utopia,* or impossibly perfect world.

One key debate in sociology today is: Are revolutions born in institutions or are they born in the minds of revolutionaries? Through the 1980s and 1990s, this was called the "Skocpol–Sewell debate" (named for Skocpol and William H. Sewell Jr.,* with whom she conducted the debate). Now, however, theories of revolution attempt to get past this debate and move toward a view where *both* theories are important. What are called "fourth generation" theories (Skocpol's are considered "third generation") attempt to understand how individual choices operate within a realm of structural constraints. Skocpol integrates these perspectives by talking about "cultural idioms."* This means that underlying structures of thought that are the same for all people, even though they might be living in different cultures, give rise to ideas that shape revolutionary change. This is not, however, referring to any one particular ideology, such as communism.

NOTES

1   Theda Skocpol, interview by Richard Snyder, "Theda Skopcol: States, Revolutions, and the Comparative Historical Imagination," in Gerardo L. Munck and Richard Snyder, *Passion, Craft, and Method in Comparative Politics* (Baltimore, MD: Johns Hopkins University Press, 2007), May 14, 2002, 650–2.

2   Skocpol, interview by Snyder, *Passion, Craft, and Method*, 656–7.

SECTION 1
INFLUENCES

THE AUTHOR AND THE HISTORICAL CONTEXT

KEY POINTS

- *States and Social Revolutions* argues that revolutions occur when particular sets of structural conditions converge.

- Theda Skocpol is an American sociologist* (someone engaged in the study of the history and functioning of society) whose education at Harvard under such figures as the political scientist Barrington Moore* profoundly shaped her approach.

- The mid-twentieth-century world was notable for the influence of revolutionary ideology.

Why Read This Text?

Theda Skocpol's *States and Social Revolution: A Comparative Analysis of France, Russia, and China* (1979) was perhaps the most significant text of the twentieth century analyzing the phenomenon of revolution. In it, Skocpol argued that several underlying conditions come together to produce revolutionary situations.

In agrarian* bureaucracies* (societies with agricultural economies and governments in which administration is an important structural feature) facing a need for modernization,* those of high status (elites) may find their interests threatened by that of modernization. If there are peasant groups dispersed around the countryside in relative autonomy, but nonetheless subjugated by a landlord class, and the state's grip over its territory is temporarily disrupted by the modernizing impulse, the peasants may rise up,

> ❝ At each evidence of [American faltering], a thrill of hope and excitement goes up through the communist world; a new jauntiness can be noted in the Moscow tread; new groups of foreign supporters climb on to what they can only view as the bandwagon of international politics; and Russian pressure increases all along the line in international affairs. ❞
>
> "X" (later revealed to be George F. Kennan, US ambassador to the Soviet Union, 1951–2), "The Sources of Soviet Conduct"

seize control of the state, and forcibly centralize and rebuild the state from the ground up.

The kinds of fundamental changes produced in these circumstances, affecting life in every way, are political *and* social. This is the definition of a social revolution,* in which the government changes, both in personnel and nature—and the way in which everyone relates to one another is altered along with it.

Skocpol's methodology was particularly influential. She uses the comparative method,* which looks at similar cases with different outcomes, and different cases with similar outcomes, in order to isolate the underlying factors that lead to those outcomes; this depends on the process of induction,* or logical inference. This sets Skocpol's study apart from those studies that focused on the psychology or ideology of the revolutionaries themselves, or that imagined the state as a mere puppet that is operated according to the interests of the dominant class.

Author's Life

Theda Skocpol was born in 1947 and grew up in a small town near Detroit, Michigan. Her parents were both high-school teachers; she has said that, while admiring them both, seeing the difficulties they dealt with in their classes she "knew [she] did not want to become a teacher at the pre-college level."[1]

She received her bachelor's degree in sociology from Michigan State University in 1969, where she graduated top of her class, before moving on to Harvard to continue her studies, supported by a generous scholarship.[2] She credits the groundbreaking nature of her work in *States and Social Revolutions* to the influence of taking a seminar under the political scientist Barrington Moore. His seminar group, famously difficult to join, "was more like a practicum"*—meaning that the students did not learn, read, and critique other theorists but, rather, actually practiced sociology.[3]

Indeed, it was for this reason that *States* emerged; if she had only read the literature, Skocpol reflected, then she would have seen that there already existed several theories of revolution that seemed "good enough." Because of Moore's teaching method, however, she was inclined to look at the evidence first, and then see if a theory naturally emerged.[4] It was in this environment, under the supervision of scholars such as the social scientists Seymour Martin Lipset,* Daniel Bell,* and George C. Homans,* that Skocpol began the dissertation that would become *States and Social Revolutions*.

Author's Background
States and Social Revolutions reflects many broader political developments of the late twentieth century, even though it discusses three revolutions—the French* (1789–99), Russian* (1917–18), and Chinese* (1921–49) Revolutions—that ended before this period.

Two international phenomena meant these revolutions were appropriate objects of study: decolonization* and the Cold War.* During the period of decolonization, colonies of the European powers in Africa, Asia, and the Caribbean claimed their independence, and global empires gave way to new states in the developing world. The Cold War was a clash of ideologically polar superpowers: the democratic, capitalist* United States and the authoritarian,* communist* Soviet Union.* The first was a system in which industry and trade were conducted for the sake of private profit, and in which liberty was prized; the other was a system in which industry and trade were managed by the state, and dissent toward the government's intervention in the life of the citizen was not tolerated.

There were two reasons, in particular, why the Cold War was of interest to those researching the sociology of revolutions. First, the Soviet Union was born of the Russian Revolution, in which the uprising led by the Bolshevik* leader Vladimir Lenin* overthrew the regime of Tsar* Nicholas II* (the Bolsheviks were a political faction composed of revolutionary workers, in the main). For Russia's new rulers, the nation, under its new communist government, would lead the world to revolution by example (or by supporting communist elements abroad).

Second, the response of the United States to the foreign policy of the Soviet Union was the strategy of "containment,"* first described by the statesman and political theorist George F. Kennan* as the encirclement of communist countries by capitalist countries, especially by sponsoring procapitalist revolutions (or countering communist revolutions) in the newly decolonized developing world.

The politics of the late twentieth century, therefore, held "revolution" to be among the most important events.

One of the best examples of both these phenomena working together was the Vietnam War.* After the French left their former colony of Indochine in Southeast Asia, the Soviet-supported communist Viet Cong* challenged its oppressive (but Western-friendly) government. The conflict, in one sense, was over the local destiny of Vietnam, in terms of whether or not the revolution would implement a communist government. But in another sense, it was also part of a global struggle.

NOTES

1   Theda Skocpol, interview by Richard Snyder, in *Passion, Craft, and Method in Comparative Politics* (Baltimore, MD: Johns Hopkins University Press, 2007), May 14, 2002, 650–2.

2   Skocpol, interview by Snyder, *Passion, Craft and Method*, 654.

3   Skocpol, interview by Snyder, *Passion, Craft and Method*, 656–7.

4   Skocpol, interview by Snyder, *Passion, Craft and Method*, 662.

ACADEMIC CONTEXT

KEY POINTS

- Sociology* has consistently debated whether to examine structure* (the large scale) or agency* (the personal).

- The German political philosopher Karl Marx* and the pioneering French sociologist Émile Durkheim* both examined broader social patterns across history and across societies.

- The political scientist Barrington Moore* argued that revolution follows a state's modernization* (technological, industrial, and social change), and the strength of the middle classes during revolution influenced the outcome; possible outcomes were democracy, fascism,* and communism.*

The Work in its Context

The context of Theda Skocpol's *States and Social Revolutions: A Comparative Analysis of France, Russia, and China* is the field of sociology. At its highest level, sociology is the study of "the social"—how society is organized, and how this enables and constrains those who live within it. One of the most important ways of understanding the ways in which social phenomena come to exist is the "functionalism" of the influential sociologist Talcott Parsons.* Parsons saw society as a complex of social institutions (religion, laws, family norms, and so forth) that served the *function* of reinforcing social cohesion and ensuring minimal conflict in the attainment of desirable ends.

Social phenomena can be understood in terms of what they "do." This is, in other words, a "grand theory"* that purports to encompass everything. The sociologist C. Wright Mills,* on the other

> ❝ It is out of the question here to discuss fully the intellectual contributions to the conception of a free society that are traceable to the historical experience of the landed upper classes. It is sufficient to remind the reader that English parliamentary democracy was very largely the creation of this class. ❞
>
> Barrington Moore, *Social Origins of Dictatorship and Democracy*

hand, argued that the idea of any "grand theory" was not a practical approach to answering the question of what it is that holds a social structure together. For him, there was no single answer, and social structures have many different strategies for social integration, and different visions for what a society should look like.[1]

Mills believes that empiricism*—attempting to analyze and understand observable phenomena rather than engaging in abstract theorizing—should be the main method of sociology. Scholars with what Mills called a "sociological imagination" are able to extract themselves from their own contexts (about what, for example, social structures "do and mean") and understand wholly different societies. That is, "the sociological imagination" aims at understanding "the inner life and the external career of a variety of individuals."[2]

The question is, then, do we understand social life as a set of structures, each with a function, and together constraining action? Or is the aim of sociology the better understanding of individuals, in which case a different approach is required?

Overview of the Field

One of history's most important theorists of revolution was the German political philosopher Karl Marx. Like the eighteenth- and nineteenth-century German philosopher Georg Hegel,* he believed that "history" was a linear process, in the course of which humanity increases its level of freedom through struggle.

Marx believed that the essence of this struggle was a matter of social class; indeed, the exploitation of the working class by the wealthy was absolutely central to his historical analysis of society. "The sum total of these relations of production," he wrote, referring to the reliance of the working class on wages paid by the capitalist* class, "constitutes the economic structure of society"; for Marx, every aspect of society and politics—including the very state itself—arose from the interests of the working class.[3]

This concept—that the state itself is nothing more than the manifestation of class interests—is core to Marxism.* Revolution, for Marx, is built into every society, as people become conscious of the way they are exploited and insist on increasing their freedom. For Marx, the French Revolution* of 1789–99 was understood as a conflict between the traditional feudal elite (who controlled the state and the tools and resources required for agricultural production) and the up and coming bourgeoisie* (the middle class, who seized control of the state). For Marx, it was critical to understand revolution as playing out, ultimately, between only two sides: the dominant class and the exploited class, with everything else as a manifestation of the interests of one of them.

Émile Durkheim* rejected what was called the "historical materialism"* of Marx, claiming it was insufficiently scientific in its analysis of the whole of society. His most notable book, *Suicide*, argued that different social structures lead to regularities in the suicide rate: that is, the suicide rate is different in every European country, but consistent inside each country. "At any given moment," Durkheim wrote, "the moral constitution of society establishes the contingent of voluntary deaths" (meaning that there are certain social structures that make suicide a more or a less likely phenomenon).[4] Durkheim argued that societies that are integrated (where people have close connections to family, society, and so forth) and regulated (where people have well-defined roles and follow social rules) make suicide less likely—unless, of course, it goes too far and people kill themselves to escape burdensome rules, for example. This is a critical insight, not because of what it says about suicide in particular, but rather for the insight that the suicide rate (a social outcome) has consistent roots in social structures.

Academic Influences

Skocpol's most important influence was Barrington Moore, whose book *The Social Origins of Dictatorship and Democracy* examines the interaction between modernization, revolution, and revolutionary outcomes (that is, the nature of the society that follows a revolution). Modernization, Moore argued, "begins with peasant revolutions that fail," but culminates "with peasant revolutions that succeed."[5] That is, modernity begins with discontent against traditional regimes and ends with the removal of those regimes.

Revolution is, however, a cross-class phenomenon and the interests of the moneyed classes, with their concerns regarding enterprise and private property, will guide peasant revolts. For Moore, revolution inevitably produces one of three societies—democratic, fascist, or communist. Fascism emphasizes pride in nationhood (often to the point of racism), military strength, and the dictatorial power of the leader.

It is the strength of the middle classes (the bourgeoisie) that determines the form the new state will take. A strong middle class produces democratic capitalism (France, England, United States); a weak middle class and a strong upper class produces fascism (the Germany and Japan of the 1940s); and a peasant revolution leads to communism (China, Russia). Whoever controls more of the state at the time of revolution determines the outcome. What was important for Skocpol was Moore's insight that existing institutions (such as the ability of the middle class to assert property rights) constrain the ability of revolutionaries to create a radically new and different state.

NOTES

1   C. Wright Mills, *The Sociological Imagination* (New York: Oxford University Press, 2000), 44.

2   Mills, *The Sociological Imagination*, 5.

3   Karl Marx, *Early Writings*, ed. Quentin Hoare (London: Penguin, 1975), 425.

4   Émile Durkheim, *Suicide: A Study in Sociology*, ed. George Simpson, trans. John A. Spaulding and George Simpson (London: Routledge, 2002), 261.

5   Barrington Moore, *Social Origins of Dictatorship and Democracy* (London: Penguin, 1991), 453.

MODULE 3
THE PROBLEM

KEY POINTS

- People asked why revolutions occur: Is revolution rooted in the revolutionaries themselves? Or do they stem from the conditions surrounding revolution?

- Most existing theories of revolutions suggested that revolutions were "voluntary"—that is, people decided to revolt and then carried out that plan.

- Skocpol rejected voluntarism, as most peasant populations do not rebel, even though they have reason; instead, she argued, we should look for conditions favorable to revolutionary situations.

Core Question

Theda Skocpol's core question in *States and Social Revolutions: A Comparative Analysis of France, Russia, and China* is: Why do revolutions occur *where* they occur, why do they occur *when* they occur, and "where are we to turn for fruitful modes of analyzing their causes and outcomes?"[1]

This question is essentially three sub-questions: What sort of evidence should be examined in order to understand where revolutions occur, when revolutions occur, and how should these revolutions be understood?

The matter was of particular relevance, especially to American scholars, because supporting noncommunist* regimes around the world was an extremely important facet of the strategy of "containment"* developed by George F. Kennan* in order to limit the foreign-policy aims of the Soviet Union,* and thereby the spread

> ❝ One irreducible characteristic of a social system is that its members hold in common a structure of values. A value structure symbolically legitimates—that is, makes morally acceptable—the particular pattern of interaction and stratification of the members of a social system. ❞
>
> Chalmers Johnson, *Revolutionary Change*

of communism. Understanding which states may have been vulnerable to revolution was a key component of American foreign policy.

"Social revolutions," Skocpol writes, "have given rise to models and ideals of enormous international impact." By this, she meant the political philosophy of liberalism* that spread around Europe in the wake of French Revolution* of 1789–99; liberalism, with its emphasis on "human rights," was instrumental to the founding of the United States—but also informed the ideological foundation of "industrial and military superpowers" such as communist Soviet Union and China.[2]

Her question arose while she was considering the injustice of the apartheid* regime in South Africa: in the face of its "blatantly oppressive" government, with legally enforced segregation of the races, "liberal justice" failed to triumph on the strength of its ideas, and "Marxist* class analysis" provided no clues as to why those who suffered failed to rise up.[3] In other words, the causes of revolutions were both critically important and mysterious.

The Participants

Skocpol examines a few competing theories of revolution. She identifies the first as "aggregate psychological theory." These are theories that hold that "many people in society"—the aggregate— "are angry"—the psychology— with a common political target.[4] The US sociologist Ted Gurr* believes this anger occurs through what he

27

calls relative deprivation—where people believe they deserve more than they have: "the potential for collective violence," he writes, "varies strongly with the intensity and scope of relative deprivation among members of a collectivity."[5] This does not mean if people are very poor, they will rebel. Rather, that they will rebel if they are poorer than they believe they ought reasonably to be.

Skocpol then turns to "political conflict theory," according to which revolution is the result of conflict between two groups.[6] The political scientist Charles Tilly* believes that revolution occurs as the result of "multiple sovereignty" in a state: "The revolutionary moment arrives" when a population (or part of it) shifts its loyalty from the government of the day to another body that it holds to be legitimate, and supports it, through taxes, declarations, military service, and so on.[7] In effect, Tilly's picture of revolution involves an alternative government gaining sufficient power and legitimacy to displace the old government.

The US political theorist Chalmers Johnson's* theory, the third attempt at theorizing revolution under discussion in *States and Social Revolutions*, focuses on what makes a revolution different from any other outbreak of mass violence.[8] Revolution occurs when the prevailing social system becomes unbearably different from the overall consensus on values; a society that values equality, for example, will violently rebel in order to change its social system if the system results in a significant concentration of wealth in the hands of a particular section of society. An outbreak of violence with the aim of changing the social system in order to bring it in line with the prevailing consensus on values is not a crime; violence not in line with the prevailing consensus on values, however, is.

The Contemporary Debate
All of these theories, Skocpol argued, shared a common conception of what revolution *is*. They all hold that "changes in a social system give

rise to grievances" provoking sections of society from industrial workers to aristocrats who now find themselves clearly at odds with the interests of their government. These grievances and interests find an alternative ideology and coalesce into a "revolutionary movement" which "fights it out with the authorities of the dominant class and if it wins" establishes a new society that reflects their ideological principles.[9]

Skocpol rejects this point of view because it cannot account for every time that mass grievances do not manage to coalesce into a revolution. Widespread popular discontent alone is not enough. This is the "voluntarist" idea of what revolution is: there is a situation that people "voluntarily" choose to change, by any means necessary. "Revolutionary crises," she argues, "are not total breakdowns in history that suddenly make anything at all possible if only it is envisaged by willful revolutionaries," but, rather, "specific possibilities and impossibilities" created by the conditions of the prerevolutionary situation.[10]

In other words, the extent to which the revolutionaries are heroic, their cause just, or they are highly motivated, matters little. What is important in determining whether or not a "revolution" will occur, and the society that revolution will produce, are the preexisting conditions. The fundamental problem is not, for Skocpol, that these frameworks prioritize structure* (regularities and rules in social interactions) over agency* (the ability of individuals to consider their options and to act after making a decision). Rather, it is that these theories all reject complexity*—they purport to provide a picture of revolution where causation proceeds neatly from one factor to another ("if x, then revolution will follow"). According to Skocpol's understanding of causes, a number of different factors work together to produce revolution.

NOTES

1   Theda Skocpol, *States and Social Revolutions: A Comparative Analysis of France, Russia, and China* (Cambridge: Cambridge University Press, 1979), 5.

2   Skocpol, *States and Social Revolutions*, 3.

3   Skocpol, *States and Social Revolutions*, xii.

4   Skocpol, *States and Social Revolutions*, 9.

5   Ted Gurr, *Why Men Rebel* (Princeton, NJ: Princeton University Press, 1970), 24.

6   Skocpol, *States and Social Revolutions*, 11.

7   Charles Tilly, *From Mobilization to Revolution* (Reading, MA: Addison Wesley, 1978), 192.

8   Chalmers Johnson, *Revolutionary Change* (Stanford, CA: Stanford University Press, 1982), 13.

9   Skocpol, *States and Social Revolutions*, 14–15.

10 Skocpol, *States and Social Revolutions*, 171.

THE AUTHOR'S CONTRIBUTION

KEY POINTS

- Skocpol aimed at a balance between a narrative history of each revolution in particular, and revolutions in general, through the comparative method.*

- The comparative method (first devised by the nineteenth-century English philosopher John Stuart Mill*) aims to find, through comparison of like and unlike cases, those factors that are causally related to the outcome under study.

- Skocpol's work had its roots in her criticism of other thinkers, especially the sociologist Barrington Moore:* she argued that modernization* must be seen as an international structural force.

Author's Aims

Theda Skocpol's *States and Social Revolutions: A Comparative Analysis of France, Russia, and China* aimed at making an argument that would "urge the reader to see old problems in a new light," specifically reorienting "our sense of what is characteristic of—and problematic about—revolutions as they have occurred historically."[1] In other words, she is trying to explain what makes revolutions distinctive, and what existing approaches to explaining them fail to address.

It is easy to mistake Skocpol's aims as formulating a general theory of revolution as opposed to merely taking an alternative approach to explaining revolutions. There are two reasons Skocpol is reluctant to generalize: the causes of revolutions always change according to the circumstances of the world at any given time, and, similarly, the categories Skocpol uses to define things such as "the state"—and the powers and responsibilities of that state—are also subject to change.[2]

> ❝ Modernization is best conceived not only as an intrasocietal process of economic development accompanied by lagging or leading changes in noneconomic institutions, but also a world–historic intersocietal process. ❞
>
> Theda Skocpol, "A Critical Review of Barrington Moore's *Social Origins of Dictatorship and Democracy*," *Social Revolutions in the Modern World*

One example of the difference is the disconnection, which emerged in the twentieth century, between a state's economic elite and its military elite. While the two were closely related in the three revolutions examined in Skocpol's book, this is no longer as important in modern bureaucratic* states (that is, states defined by the importance of administration). The distinction between a general approach and a general theory is important, especially in relation to *States and Social Revolutions*; Skocpol is restricting herself to analyzing what can be deduced empirically through comparison, rather than theorizing. Instead of specifying a general answer to every instance of the question "Why did this revolution occur?" she is suggesting an altogether new approach.

Approach

One of the most distinctive aspects of the book is its use of comparative historical analysis on an enormous scale. This method, in which different historical periods are compared to better understand the relationship between causes and effects, has its roots in the work of the nineteenth-century English philosopher John Stuart Mill on causal inference* (the process of examining chains of events so as to understand which factors in the chain led to which outcomes).

Essentially, imagine two processes leading to the same outcome but with only one factor in common (*factor A*). Then imagine two processes that have nearly everything in common except for *factor A*, but that do not lead to the same outcome.[3] In this case, *factor A* can be inferred to be the cause of (or certainly something contributing to) the outcome.

Following this method, Skocpol analyzes three cases—the French,* the Chinese,* and the Russian* revolutions—where a similar set of circumstances led to social revolutions. She also examines the Prussian Revolution* of 1848 (an uprising centered on the city of Berlin in what is today Germany) and the Meiji Restoration* in Japan in 1868, neither of which produced social revolutions.[4] These negative cases, while more numerous, are not analyzed in the same depth.

The goal of the comparative methodology, as opposed to descriptive history, is not merely to outline processes, or to describe the trajectories of past events, but to use similarities and differences between cases to isolate and validate the important cause (or causes) of an event (revolution, in this case).[5] This is not perfectly akin to science, where we can isolate and test, for example, the effect of a given pill on a certain condition, because social phenomena are too complex. The method makes some major assumptions about what factors could be relevant that make the method less exacting than so-called "hard science." It is not possible to make a perfect list of every single aspect of prerevolutionary France, for example, meaning that it becomes inevitable that an educated guess has to be made as to which ones are most likely to be relevant.[6]

Contribution in Context

Skocpol's engagement with other theorists, especially her mentor Barrington Moore, was very important indeed to her writing *States and Social Revolutions*. In a review of Moore's *Social Origins of Dictatorship and Democracy* (1966), Skocpol writes that, for Moore, the "commercial impulse" is "the motor of social change" driving agrarian* (farming) societies to transform into industrial societies through revolution as it undermines "agrarian bureaucracy."[7] Skocpol's main problem with Moore is that his analysis remains too grounded within societies; the "commercial impulse" exists everywhere, and moves within societies as a kind of indefinable force.[8]

One of Skocpol's key criticisms of Moore's analysis is that many of the fascist* regimes he considers (especially the nineteenth century elite-directed revolutions "from above" in Germany and Japan that led to fascist states emerging in the twentieth century) are so far removed from the revolutions that allegedly caused them that one might think explanations may be more readily found elsewhere. Skocpol suggests that fascist and communist* governments (which remain repressive) "could be interpreted as attempts also to insulate national economies from a world economy" that was becoming mature enough to cut off opportunities for "native" industry to develop, and "require instead that politics be put in command" of all economic forms of life "if the substance of national sovereignty were to be retained."[9]

NOTES

1   Theda Skocpol, *States and Social Revolutions: A Comparative Analysis of France, Russia, and China* (Cambridge: Cambridge University Press, 1979), xi.

2   Skocpol, *States and Social Revolutions*, 288.

3   John Stuart Mill, *A System of Logic: Volume I* (London: John W. Parker, 1851), 462.

4   Skocpol, *States and Social Revolutions*, 37.

5   Skocpol, *States and Social Revolutions*, 38.

6   Skocpol, *States and Social Revolutions*, 38.

7   Theda Skocpol, *Social Revolutions in the Modern World* (Cambridge: Cambridge University Press, 1994), 44.

8   Skocpol, *Social Revolutions in the Modern World*, 46.

9   Skocpol, *Social Revolutions in the Modern World*, 47.

SECTION 2
IDEAS

MODULE 5
MAIN IDEAS

KEY POINTS

- The contrasts between "structure"* and "agency"* (two approaches to sociological analysis, the first concerned with the composition of society, the other with the behavior of individuals) and the contrast between the "international" and the "domestic" are critical for Skocpol.

- Agrarian* autocracies*—agricultural societies ruled by a dictatorial figure—face threats from abroad, forcing them to modernize;* the conflict between members of the higher social classes that this provokes gives citizens opportunities for revolutionary change.

- For some, the book's relatively scientific organization makes it an overly rigid text.

Key Themes

Two themes in Theda Skocpol's *States and Social Revolutions: A Comparative Analysis of France, Russia, and China* are critical: the contrast between structure and agency, and between the international and the domestic.

In brief, "structure" refers to the effects of things such as social class and economy—factors external to individuals that affect a society in certain ways ("social outcomes"); "agency" refers to the influence of individuals themselves over these social outcomes. We can think of this as a river. If we imagine the will of individual people to be a river, its banks are "structure"; they direct it independent of its flowing. Skocpol chooses to focus on structure because, historically, revolutions do not conform to the ideological vision of any one group contributing to that revolution, and complexity* can be made sense of "only by focusing on the institutionally determined situations and relations of

> **❝** Social revolutions are rapid, basic transformations of a society's state and class structures; and they are accompanied and in part carried through by class-based revolts from below. Social revolutions are set apart from other sorts of conflicts and transformative processes above all by the combination of two coincidences: the coincidence of societal structural change with class upheaval. **❞**
>
> Theda Skocpol, *States and Social Revolutions: A Comparative Analysis of France, Russia, and China*

groups within society and upon the interrelations of societies" within the international structure.[1] That is: a revolution must be understood by considering the structures (class, economy, and so on) that define the society undergoing revolution, and the nature of that society's relationship to other societies in the international system.

Skocpol's analysis is "structural" because she argues that revolutionary outcomes correspond to *patterns of relationships between competing groups* rather than to the desires of any particular group.

The second key theme is the contrast between the international and the domestic. The structure of international relations between states can be defined as one of roughly equal but competing entities (nations), aiming to achieve influence over one another. There are structures of dominance in the international system (some states are more powerful than others), but nations are separate. Within the domestic sphere, on the other hand, different social groups (often separated by classes, whether peasants, landlords, or rulers) negotiate their interests *within* a web of institutions. "An existing economy and class structure," Skocpol argues, "condition and influence a given state structure and the activities of the rulers."[2]

States and Social Revolutions aims to show how dynamics between these two systems lead to complete and irreversible change.

Exploring the Ideas

A "social revolution"* is a unique concept. These revolutions are "rapid, basic transformations of a society's state and class structures."[3] This means the entire social and political order is fundamentally changed: social classes are torn apart, the very basic premises of political association are rewritten so that a monarchy,* for example, might become a republic* with the end of hereditary rule by kings and queens. Second, Skocpol identifies social revolution (unlike, say, riots or rebellions) with success: for a social revolution to qualify as such, it *must* involve a total transformation of social and political life, meaning it *must* be successful.

So how do we get social revolution? Within the realm of the international, states compete with one another, both economically and militarily. One of the most important dimensions of state competition—importantly for France, China, and Russia—involves modernization relative to other states. All three of these states had primarily agrarian,* relatively backward, and nonindustrialized economies, and relatively weaker militaries than important competitors.[4] In the examples Skocpol gives, social revolution occurred "through the impact of defeat in total war with more developed powers," as in the case of Russia, or turmoil at home "through the reaction of politically powerful landed upper classes against monarchial attempts to mobilize resources or impose reforms (as in the case of France of China)" allowing responses to international military competition.[5]

Having understood the place of the revolutionary state within the international order, the specific revolution must be understood in the context of the specific state. If the international system is the structure that presents different states with different problems (increased competition, for example), the state is the structure within which those problems are solved, through things such as modernization and reforms in administration. The state is a set of institutions (such as tax authorities, military authorities, domestic coercive authorities like the police) that relates *both* to other states *and* to dominant and subordinate social classes within its borders. Essentially, states respond in part to pressures abroad by making changes at home.

Considering the French,* Russian,* and Chinese* revolutions, while these changes "may or may not be successfully implemented," they can "create a contradictory clash of interests between the state and the existing dominant class."[6] In France, the ruling Bourbon monarchy* raised taxes on everyone, including the wealthy, in an attempt to bolster its standing against other, more powerful and wealthy European states. The "landed commercial upper classes stood to lose wealth and power if central authorities succeeded in their rationalizing reforms," Skocpol writes; in other words, reforms executed by the autocratic governments of her study with the aim of competing more effectively with other nations were counterproductive to national stability.[7]

It is this that creates the space for social revolutions to occur: and those who drive the engine of the revolution are peasants. "Peasants are … primary agricultural cultivators," meaning farmers, "who must, because of political and cultural marginality," be forced to live under unjust regimes of tax, theft, rents, discrimination, and so on.[8] For this reason, Skocpol thinks peasants *always* have sufficient grounds for revolt. When peasants are able to organize and mobilize themselves (meaning they arrange their own day-to-day affairs among themselves and feel solidarity together), they can seize the moment of "hiatus of governmental supervision and sanctions" in order to rise up against the landlord class (rather than, for example, the king, emperor, or tsar*).[9]

Language and Expression

States and Social Revolutions enjoyed a broad impact and continues to be read today. The sociologist Jeff Goodwin* credits this, at least in part, to the fact that it was "a well-researched, brilliantly argued, carefully crafted, and clearly written book on an important subject."[10] A core part of the strength of the argument was Skocpol's scientific, rather than personal, perspective. That is, her argument is laid out and organized on the basis of a hypothesis made in the first chapter, and tested through considerations of international pressure, domestic reform and resistance, and peasant uprisings.

However, as Goodwin goes on to argue, this scientific, theory-testing approach led to some widespread misunderstanding of *States and Social Revolutions*, generally in the form of oversimplification. It is tempting, he argues, for writers in the field to use "Skocpol, 1979" to present an overly simplified vision of revolutions in which ideas are irrelevant, and only states matter, when Skocpol was actually presenting a more nuanced argument about the *interaction* between states and substate groups, or ideas and structures.[11]

NOTES

1   Theda Skocpol, *States and Social Revolutions: A Comparative Analysis of France, Russia, and China* (Cambridge: Cambridge University Press, 1979), 18.

2   Skocpol, *States and Social Revolutions*, 30.

3   Skocpol, *States and Social Revolutions*, 4.

4   Skocpol, *States and Social Revolutions*, 23.

5   Skocpol, *States and Social Revolutions*, 50.

6   Skocpol, *States and Social Revolutions*, 31.

7   Skocpol, *States and Social Revolutions*, 81.

8   Skocpol, *States and Social Revolutions*, 115.

9   Skocpol, *States and Social Revolutions*, 112.

10   Jeff Goodwin, "Review: How to Become a Dominant American Social Scientist: The Case of Theda Skocpol," *Contemporary Sociology* 25, no. 3 (1996): 293.

11   Goodwin, "Review," 294.

MODULE 6
SECONDARY IDEAS

KEY POINTS

- Rationalization*—changing the way things are done to make them more efficient, predictable, and impersonal according to the principle of "means–ends" logic—is important to the form that postrevolutionary states eventually take.

- The more a social and political order needed to be destroyed, the more centralized and totalizing the new state will be; following the French Revolution* the French military could be reformed; following the Chinese* and Russian* Revolutions, it needed to be destroyed.

- For Skocpol, revolutionary ideology is a necessary part of revolution, even if it is not the most important factor in the analysis of causes and effects. This assumption has been heavily criticized.

Other Ideas
Despite the similarities in the conditions that gave rise to the revolutions in France, Russia, and China, the second part of Theda Skocpol's *States and Social Revolutions: A Comparative Analysis of France, Russia, and China* considers different aspects of the revolutionary situations in all three countries. It considers, too, the ways in which these things constrained the decisions of revolutionaries in the creation of their new states. This is an important way in which Skocpol brings "agency"* (the importance of what people believe and the decisions they make) back into her "structural"* theory (which focuses on social structures such as class and economics).

> ❝ In each New Regime, there was much greater popular incorporation into the state-run affairs of the nation. And the new state organizations forged during the Revolutions were more centralized and rationalized than those of the Old Regime. Hence they were more potent within society and more powerful and autonomous over and against competitors within the international states system. ❞
>
> Theda Skocpol, *States and Social Revolutions: A Comparative Analysis of France, Russia, and China*

One of the ways in which the revolutions were similar is that they aimed to create strong, centralized states that could compete more effectively in the international system. This is the theme of rationalization, and it finds its root in the writing of the pioneering German sociologist Max Weber.* Weber sees rationalization as the "methodical attainment of a definitely given and practical end by means of an increasingly precise calculation of adequate means"; it was necessarily connected with bureaucratization*—the process by which a society comes to be defined by the administration that allows it to function.[1]

Rationalization, in this context, is a matter of reconsidering what the state aims to attain (greater farm production, for example, or industrialization), and organizing the resources of the state in the most effective possible pursuit of these objectives by placing authority in the hands of professionals with limited, well-defined responsibility. So instead of investing responsibility for military recruitment, say, in the hands of a local lord, a bureaucracy decides exactly how many people are needed, from where, and with which skill sets, and then carries out the plan. Ultimately, bureaucratization is about replacing human thought and judgment with technology and rules.

Exploring the Ideas

Skocpol opens by reminding us that "peasant revolts against landlords" led to the transformation of "class relations" in societies with agricultural economies, and "autocratic … monarchies* gave way to bureaucratic* … national states."[2] However, one key difference between the French Revolution on the one hand and the Chinese and Russian Revolutions on the other is the emergence of communist* "party-led state organizations" that assumed totalitarian* control over every aspect of life in the latter two, as opposed to a "professional-bureaucratic state," and "national markets and capitalist* private property"[3] in the case of France.

In France, Skocpol writes, the state was encumbered by "institutionalized and politically guaranteed local, provincial, occupational, and estate rights and corporate bodies"; that is, people were allowed to buy their offices and run them for their own profits according to a complicated and irrational system of rules that meant most people (peasants *and* the educated classes) lost out.[4] The revolution ended up strengthening the state apparatus, ridding it of "medieval rubbish" that led to inefficiencies in rule, production, administration, and so forth. She gives the example of the military organization, where leadership positions had (under the old regime) gone to nobleman, who were primarily farmers and local administrators; centralization and rationalization of the state military meant that professional "military officers were provided with salaries adequate to allow them to become full time, career specialists," and the nobility drifted into irrelevance, as far as real power and influence was concerned.[5]

In many ways, this was made necessary by the wars of the French leader Napoleon Bonaparte,* who needed to rationalize a military that had formerly been as important for reinforcing the social status of the nobility as it was for fighting wars effectively. These changes are emblematic of an entire state being made more efficient and more professional.

The Russian Revolution produced a much stronger state because the Tsarist monarchical regime it overthrew defined so absolutely all social orders in Russia (more so than France), and because it collapsed so completely in 1917 that society, in effect, collapsed with it and needed to be rebuilt. The Bolshevik* revolutionaries—members of an action group key in instigating the revolution—needed to consolidate power rapidly throughout a predominantly agricultural society with few cities to give rise to organized revolutionary groups.[6] Driving the rapid industrialization that was needed to bring Russia into the twentieth century, then, was a "narrow and precarious political basis in a predominantly agrarian society" with a peasantry, who were not revolutionary insiders, being forcibly harnessed.[7]

Like the French Revolution, the Russian Revolution centralized and modernized* the nation rapidly in order to defeat counterrevolutionary elements inside and outside the country. Russia, however, became a more totalitarian state because the former Tsarist state was so much more integral to every aspect of society than the French state. Returning to the army, for example, the French professionalized and modernized an existing military, whereas the Russians needed to create one from scratch.

Overlooked

It is often argued that Skocpol is completely uninterested in the role of revolutionaries and their ideas in causing social revolutions, favoring instead the role of structure. But though Skocpol's account of the role of revolutionary ideology* is limited, it is by no means nonexistent. Revolutionary ideologies—justification for revolution, and visions of the ideal society that will come to replace the existing order after the revolution—are "undoubtedly necessary ingredients in the great social revolutions." But the critical point for Skocpol is that they are not sufficient *in themselves* to predict the outbreak of revolution or its resulting society.[8]

Revolutionary ideology is necessary because, at least for the three social revolutions under study, they were creeds that affected all the citizens of their states, encouraging people from different regions and backgrounds to work together and to convert people to the universal cause. Moreover, the revolutionary ideologies provided justifications for revolutions. In the French Revolution, this took the form of the belief held by the political faction known as the Jacobins* that revolution was in accordance with the "general will" of society. In the case of Russia and China, it was the Marxist–Leninist* belief that the creation of a "classless society" was worth every sacrifice.[9]

Although ideologies provided key justifications for the revolutionaries, Skocpol gives them only a limited role: revolutions are not moments of "unlimited openness" where the beliefs of the bold are implemented perfectly. Instead, structural conditions cause "practical detours on the road to power," meaning ideologies are almost always implemented imperfectly.[10]

NOTES

1   Max Weber, *The Protestant Ethic and the Spirit of Capitalism* (New York: Scribner's, 1958), 293.

2   Theda Skocpol, *States and Social Revolutions: A Comparative Analysis of France, Russia, and China* (Cambridge: Cambridge University Press, 1979), 161.

3   Skocpol, *States and Social Revolutions*, 162.

4   Skocpol, *States and Social Revolutions*, 179.

5   Skocpol, *States and Social Revolutions*, 197.

6   Skocpol, *States and Social Revolutions*, 231.

7   Skocpol, *States and Social Revolutions*, 233.

8   Skocpol, *States and Social Revolutions*, 170.

9   Skocpol, *States and Social Revolutions*, 170.

10 Skocpol, *States and Social Revolutions*, 171.

MODULE 7
ACHIEVEMENT

KEY POINTS

- Skocpol's study was questioned both for its theoretical and methodological rigor.

- The year *States and Social Revolutions* was published, 1979, revolutions broke out in Iran and Nicaragua that did not conform to its theory. The book nonetheless remained immensely popular.

- The sociologist Barbara Geddes* suggests the book was limited in its analysis because of "selection on the dependent variable"*—that is, Skocpol selected her examples (France, China, Russia, Germany, Japan) precisely because they all experienced revolutions, thereby introducing a bias into her analysis.

Assessing the Argument

In *States and Social Revolutions: A Comparative Analysis of France, Russia, and China*, Theda Skocpol intended to explain one of the most important political phenomena of the modern age—revolutions—as the products of structural* factors in a society, such as social class and the nature of the nation's economy. Her argument was supported by evidence that could be verified by observation (that is, empirical* evidence), rather than on more speculative arguments about, say, how people were provoked to revolution by feelings of deprivation.

Yet if the theory she proposed was internally consistent (in that it does not contradict itself, or rely on *obviously* implausible assumptions), what is less certain is the extent to which her theory was, indeed, properly empirical. Some critics suggested her study was insufficiently rigorous theoretically; Skocpol herself wondered if her work were

> **❝** In France, Russia, and China, class conflicts ... were pivotal during the revolutionary interregnums. But both the occurrence of the revolutionary situations in the first place and the nature of the New Regimes that emerged from the revolutionary conflicts depended fundamentally upon the structures of state organizations and their partially autonomous and dynamic relationships to domestic class and political forces, as well as their positions in relation to other states abroad. **❞**
>
> Theda Skocpol, *States and Social Revolutions: A Comparative Analysis of France, Russia, and China*

rigorous enough in its *method*. "There may have been aspects of revolutions that I could have tested statistically," she stated. Ultimately, though, she decided that she was not engaged in a project of determining, down to the nearest percentage point, the extent to which any area could be seen as prone to revolution. Rather, she was engaged in a project of identifying trends, one in which extreme methodological rigor would have been unlikely to have improved her argument. Her goal, that is to say, was a new kind of theory of revolution. "We now," she said, "have powerful knowledge about what accounts for revolutions and their absence," and it was not achieved by "leaping to the most general questions" of "big" theory, but rather by looking at the general trends of a small number of deliberately selected cases.[1]

Achievement in Context

In 1979, the year *States and Social Revolutions* was published, two further revolutions occurred. The Iranian Revolution* deposed the corrupt government of the monarch Mohammad Reza Shah

Pahlavi,* and led to the founding of the Islamic Republic* of Iran. "Iran's dominant class," wrote Skocpol in a paper that sought to explain the revolution, "consisted of state bureaucrats,* foreign capitalist* investors, and domestic capitalists closely tied by patronage and regulation to the state," meaning the royal family.[2] Iran was a state dependent on oil exports in which a small elite gained conspicuous wealth and the armed forces were lavishly funded.[3]

While the revolution enjoyed wide support, it was led by urban workers and an emerging middle class rather than village-based peasants, who not only lacked the solidarity required for a revolution but, in an economy based on petro-chemicals rather than agriculture, could never have expected to exercise much leverage.[4] The revolution forced Skocpol to reconsider her argument about the role of ideas in revolution, as the Shia* branch of Islam was key both to the coming of the revolution and the form the new state took.

The Iranian Revolution, she argued, was "made through a set of cultural and organizational forms thoroughly socially embedded in the urban [places] that became the centers of popular resistance to the Shah." Her argument specifically focused on the "moral symbols and forms of social communication offered by Shia Islam."[5] In sum, the revolution occurred because Iran's autocratic* government and dependence on oil revenues made it vulnerable to a "self-made" revolution led by urban workers unified by Shia Islam.

Limitations

The sociologist Barbara Geddes* argued that Skocpol's theory in *States and Social Revolutions* is limited by case selection,* which introduces an inherent bias into the argument. Specifically, she said the theory suffers from a flaw in statistical analysis called "selection on the dependent variable."[6] This means that Skocpol selected her examples (France, China, Russia, Germany, Japan) precisely because they all experienced revolutions.

But, Geddes asked, what if we choose a randomly selected set of countries? Would we then find Skocpol's argument confirmed or refuted? Statistical logic suggests that a theoretical statement is valid if the outcome of the model (even if it is demonstrated through a sample of the whole) should correspond, roughly, to the whole population. For Geddes, the theory should ideally test the entire population of villages characterized by the underlying features that make a state vulnerable to revolution, registering "village autonomy and a dominant class with an independent economic base and access to political power." It would then be possible to determine to what extent an external threat would produce the revolutionary "spark."[7]

In practice, this would be impractical, requiring detailed knowledge of every single country in the world from 1789, the date of the French Revolution,* to the present day, on the basis that moments when revolutions *do not* take place are as important for causal inference as moments when revolutions *do* take place. Geddes suggests, instead, that Skocpol should have looked at Latin American countries—selected because they "approximate Skocpol's description of the autonomous … village structure [characterized by solidarity] that makes possible peasants' participation in revolution"—and compared them to her cases.

Did an external threat spark these countries into revolution as Skocpol's theory claims would happen?[8] Geddes suggests that, by and large, Latin American countries *do not* conform to Skocpol's theory. "Seven instances of extreme military threat," she writes, "failed to lead to revolution," and "two revolutions [were] not preceded by any unusual degree of external competition or threat." She is able to find only one case that conforms to Skocpol's theory.[9]

NOTES

1   Theda Skocpol, interview by Richard Snyder, in *Passion, Craft, and Method in Comparative Politics* (Baltimore: Johns Hopkins University Press, 2007), May 14, 2002, 689.

2   Theda Skocpol, "Rentier State and Shi'a Islam in the Iranian Revolution," *Theory and Society* 11, no. 3 (1982): 265.

3   Skocpol, "Rentier State," 280.

4   Skocpol, "Rentier State," 270.

5   Skocpol, "Rentier State," 275.

6   Barbara Geddes, "How the Cases You Choose Affect the Answers You Get: Selection Bias in Comparative Politics," *Political Analysis* 2, no. 1 (1990): 141.

7   Geddes, "How the Cases You Choose Affect the Answers You Get," 143.

8   Geddes, "How the Cases You Choose Affect the Answers You Get," 144.

9   Geddes, "How the Cases You Choose Affect the Answers You Get," 145.

PLACE IN THE AUTHOR'S WORK

KEY POINTS

- While *States and Social Revolutions* was Skocpol's first major publication, her body of work went on to encompass a number of other topics.

- Skocpol's work was, for the most part, highly empirical and used the scientific method; furthermore, much of her work put states at the center of the action.

- *States and Social Revolutions* remains significant in the fields of sociology* and international relations.*

Positioning

Although Theda Skocpol published *States and Social Revolutions: A Comparative Analysis of France, Russia, and China* in 1979, it began life as her dissertation in Harvard. It was her first major published work. But while she would continue pursuing this theme, if only sporadically, throughout her career, it was not to be her primary focus.

Her ambitions grew from the interpretation of evidence to setting the agenda within her discipline. Her next book, *Vision and Method in Historical Sociology* (1984), attempted to reorient and compare all the major methodologies of historical sociology: "a methodological bibliography" that would help make sociology a more standardized discipline, with agreed methods for solving what were agreed to be problems.[1] *Bringing the State Back In* (1985), a volume cowritten with the sociologists Peter B. Evans* and Dietrich Rueschemeyer,* merged many of the concerns of sociology with international relations. The book aimed to argue how states, defined as "organizations claiming control over territories and people," can set and pursue goals

> 66 States conceived as organizations claiming control over territories and people may formulate and pursue goals that are not simply reflective of the demands or interests of social groups, classes, or society. This is what is usually meant by 'state autonomy.' 99
>
> Theda Skocpol, *Bringing the State Back In*

autonomously (as opposed to goals that reflect interest groups, classes, or society itself).[2] This autonomy—capacity to act as a sovereign nation—is a matter of concern to the international realm, where states interact (primarily) with other states, but in the domestic realm also, where states act within their own societies.

It was this second concept—the state as an actor within domestic politics—that actually defined much of Skocpol's later output, especially in relation to the formulation of social policy.* Her book *Protecting Soldiers and Mothers*, published in 1992, discussed the formation of the American welfare state in the era of the American Civil War* (1861–5). Her work through the 1990s and 2000s brings her analysis of domestic economy policy forward, as she examines the failure to extend social policy further (*Boomerang: Health Care Reform and the Turn Against Government*), and even more recently, beyond "the state" to look at social movements within America. *What a Mighty Power We Can Be*, published in 2006, demonstrates the role played in the Civil Rights Movement*—the struggle for equal social and political rights for black Americans—by African American community engagement groups such as charitable organizations.

Integration

Skocpol's body of work does not tell a single story. In fact, it is almost intentionally fragmented. "Soon after *States and Social Revolutions* appeared," Skocpol said, "I reached a point where I did not want to write about revolutions anymore." She turned instead to new problems.[3]

A few things, however, remained consistent for much of Skocpol's career, not least her use of the comparative method* (especially in her work on social policy). According to the comparative method, the researcher compares different historical cases or examples of certain phenomena in order to determine what might have caused a particular outcome. Just like Skocpol argued against "grand" theorists (especially Marxists)* that revolution was an inevitable part of modernisation, she also argued against the point of view that the welfare state was an inevitabile part of the same process. She felt that the welfare state,* too, was a product of particular circumstances.*[4] She refers to her approach as "structured* polity."

The "structured polity" approach requires the examination of four factors:

- State and political party organizations "through which politicians pursue policy initiatives"
- "[The] effects of political institutions on ... social groups that become involved in the politics of social policymaking"
- "The fit ... between the goals and capacities of various politically active groups"
- "The ways in which previously established social policies affect subsequent politics."[5]

This approach sees the state and its administrators as playing a key role in the establishment of domestic policy, and as an autonomous actor (that is, a body that acts independently). Skocpol's argument, as she goes on to recount how the welfare state emerged in the United States, also refers back to *States and Social Revolutions*. "Longstanding political structures," such as a strong sense of federalism* (a system of government in which administrative power is shared between different levels of government, as in Germany where a federation of states is under national government control) contributed to preventing the emergence of widespread "class consciousness"—a knowledge of one's place in the social hierarchy—in the United States, as it did in Europe.[6] However, groups that could claim solidarity, such as women's groups, could encourage broad political support.[7]

Significance

States and Social Revolutions was Skocpol's most important work, and continues to be her best known. It was for *States and Social Revolutions* that Skocpol landed on *Foreign Policy*'s list of top ten books on international relations by women. Despite being written originally as a sociological* treatise, it found its greatest impact in international relations. Even though *States* is "primarily a work of comparative historical sociology," writes the sociologist Stephen Walt,* "Skocpol's pathbreaking work also emphasizes the role of international pressures in driving great revolutions," and is a work "to be reckoned with."[8] Among specialists in different disciplines, especially those studying social connectedness and welfare states, however, she is known for her significant contributions there. *Bringing the State Back In*, for example, still appears on undergraduate reading lists.

In fact, if one sees much of Skocpol's career as outlining the ways in which "the state," long relegated to merely an arena over which different actors squabble, is a meaningful concept, then her overall project can be seen as highly significant, and attuned to the same goal. "The most important accomplishment of *States and Social Revolutions*," writes Skocpol, was "to have successfully hit scholars over the head with 'the obvious,'" namely, "the centrality of state power and coercive organizations in all revolutions"—and indeed, in all facets of life.[9]

NOTES

1   Theda Skocpol, interview by Richard Snyder, in *Passion, Craft, and Method in Comparative Politics* (Baltimore: Johns Hopkins University Press, 2007), May 14, 2002, 672.

2   Theda Skocpol, "Bringing the State Back In: Strategies of Analysis in Current Research," in *Bringing the State Back In*, ed. Peter B. Evans, Dietrich Rueschemeyer, and Theda Skocpol (Cambridge: Cambridge University Press, 1985), 9.

3   Skocpol, interview by Snyder, *Passion, Craft, and Method in Comparative Politics*, 676.

4   Theda Skocpol, *Protecting Soldiers and Mothers: The Political Origins of Social Policy in the United States* (Cambridge, MA: Belknap Press, 1992), 14.

5   Skocpol, *Protecting Soldiers and Mothers*, 41.

6   Skocpol, *Protecting Soldiers and Mothers*, 50.

7   Skocpol, *Protecting Soldiers and Mothers*, 60.

8   Stephen Walt, "Top Ten IR Books by Women," *Foreign Policy*, April 14 2009, accessed October 27, 2015, http://foreignpolicy.com/2009/04/14/top-ten-ir-books-by-women/?wp_login_redirect=0.

9   Theda Skocpol, *Social Revolutions in the Modern World* (Cambridge: Cambridge University Press, 1994), 8.

SECTION 3
IMPACT

THE FIRST RESPONSES

KEY POINTS

- *States and Social Revolutions* was criticized for being overly dependent on induction,* and for limiting the role of the ideology to those engaged in revolution.

- Skocpol rejected the first criticism, but brought the other on board to broaden her conception of the role of ideology.

- *States and Social Revolutions* is a notable example of a sociological analysis investigating structure* (things such as class and the nature of the economy). It emphasizes third-generation revolutionary theory.*

Criticism

Theda Skocpol's *States and Social Revolutions: A Comparative Analysis of France, Russia, and China* was widely read and discussed on publication; the first criticism came from a Marxist,* the British sociologist* Michael Burawoy.* Essentially, he argued that Skocpol "induces her structural theory from facts," whereas the Marxist revolutionary and theorist of revolution Leon Trotsky* "situates himself within a Marxist *research program** and *deduces* the direction of history."[1] To put it simply, Burawoy is suggesting that Skocpol has decided on a collection of facts to examine, and then used a process of induction to turn a pattern of outcomes implied by those facts into a general idea of how the world works; the orthodox Marxist approach would be to begin with the assumption that history is advanced above all by class struggle, and to make predictions through a process of deduction,* using premises that are definitely true that account for this.

The sociologist Michael Hechter* makes what is ultimately a similar argument to Burawoy, although replacing "Marxism" with

> ❝ Ideology must be seen neither as the mere reflex of material class relations nor as mere 'ideas' which 'intellectuals' hold about society. Rather, ideologies inform the structure of institutions, the nature of social cooperation and conflict, and the attitudes and predispositions of the population. All social relations are at the same time ideological relations, and all explicit ideological discourse is a form of social action. ❞
>
> William H. Sewell Jr., "Ideologies and Social Revolutions: Reflections on the French Case"

"rational choice." His argument is that Skocpol fails to specify a theory of the motivations of individual actors; she relies, he claims, on "narrative accounts to specify the interests of actors"—which are often contradictory.

The sociologist William H. Sewell Jr.* argues that Skocpol's rejection of ideology* (that is, the idea that the ideology of a revolution can help predict its outcome) is an "extreme position and a very difficult one to sustain."[2] He suggests that Skocpol's treatment of ideology—as the "blueprint" for change held by identifiable individuals—is an unfair simplification.[3] Ideology, he argues, should be seen as a structural factor in constraining and enabling revolution, rather than merely an idea that certain revolutionaries happen to hold. "An ideological structure," Sewell argues, "is not some self-consistent 'blueprint' but the outcome of the often contradictory or antagonistic action of a large number of actors"—that is, it is the ideas that underpin every institution, and it is the unconscious agreement that gives the revolutionaries common cause.[4] Rather than a belief about society, then, ideology is what underpins it; it is not held by any one person (or group), but is a kind of "anonymous, collective" idea.[5] In essence, "ideology" is seen as a cultural system: it is both the commonly unstated idea about what is worth discussing and the basic assumptions on which society is built.

Responses

Skocpol responded to Burawoy, Hechter, and Sewell in the concluding chapter of 1994's *Social Revolutions in the Modern World*. She suggests that all three criticisms share a common element: they call "for other styles of scholarship" to replace comparative* historical analysis.[6] For the former two, Skocpol suggests it is not a problem that she did not "theoretically explicate the empirical* regularities" in the book, meaning she did not start with a theory of human action (like Marxism or rational choice).[7] For her, this is mistakenly narrow, and not a criticism that builds on her work; it is a rejection of her method rather than the proposal of a viable alternative.

Sewell's criticism, on the other hand, Skocpol takes on board. She accepts that her treatment of ideology did not give it its due. She thinks, however, that Sewell's argument—that ideology as a "cultural system" held by everyone and no one, rather than identifiable individuals—is still too broad. She distinguishes between "ideologies" as systems of ideas used by identifiable groups to further their aims, and "cultural idioms," which are "longer-term, more anonymous, and less partisan."[8] We draw on cultural idioms in the production of ideology, as the underlying assumptions of what is possible and desirable.

Skocpol brings the role of ideas back to her analysis in a similar way to her method of bringing in class conflict: by considering how they are related to the breakdown of the state and the centralization of power. "We need," she writes, "to examine the possibilities [for consolidating state power, and the way they have] interacted with the specific ideas and modes of political action available to particular group."[9]

Conflict and Consensus

According to the sociologist Jack Goldstone,* *States and Social Revolutions* moved revolutionary scholarship from a psychologically focused second-generation analysis to a third generation focusing on social structures. The end of the long period of global tension known as the Cold War* and the revolutions in places such as Iran* and Nicaragua* of the late 1970s and 1980s led, Goldstone wrote, to three major changes in the structural study of revolutions. First, theories were being applied to an increasingly diverse set of cases, especially the anticommunist* uprisings that occurred as the Soviet Union* disintegrated. Second, ideology and agency* (the capacity of individuals to act) were being brought back in to explain the differences between kinds of revolution. Third, many of the processes underlying revolutions (mass mobilization, confrontation with authorities, broad-based change) also underlay social movements such as the struggle for rights for women and minorities.[10]

Goldstone argued that, given the increasing complexity of revolutionary situations, Skocpol's theory needs to be turned on its head: instead of revolutions being treated as the outcome of interest, with the factors of interest being those that contribute to instability, it must "treat stability as problematic and focus on conditions that sustain regimes over time."[11] Goldstone thinks there are three conditions for stability: governments that are perceived as effective and just; elites that are unanimous in support of the regime; popular groups with a reliable, acceptable standard of living.[12] Ultimately, the most important move Goldstone suggests as the "fourth generation" of revolutionary scholarship is the move to make the categories of revolution less "fixed," including what a revolution is.

Ultimately, the debate between structure and agency in revolutions (sometimes called the Skocpol–Sewell debate) has defined the discipline; the ways in which boundaries are being pushed in the so-called fourth-generation analysis is by trying to unite structure and agency rather than by asserting the importance of one over the other.

NOTES

1   Michael Burawoy, "Two Methods in Search of Science: Skocpol versus Trotsky," *Theory and Society* 18, no. 6 (1989): 779.

2   William H. Sewell Jr., "Ideologies and Social Revolutions: Reflections on the French Case," *The Journal of Modern History* 57, no. 1 (1985): 59.

3   Sewell, "Ideologies and Social Revolutions," 60.

4   Sewell, "Ideologies and Social Revolutions," 61.

5   Sewell, "Ideologies and Social Revolutions," 61.

6   Theda Skocpol, *Social Revolutions in the Modern World* (Cambridge: Cambridge University Press, 1994), 318.

7   Skocpol, *Social Revolutions in the Modern World,* 323.

8   Theda Skocpol, "Cultural Idioms and Political Ideologies in the Revolutionary Reconstruction of State Power: A Rejoinder to Sewell," *The Journal of Modern History* 57, no. 1 (1985): 91.

9   Skocpol, "Cultural Idioms and Political Ideologies," 93.

10 Jack A. Goldstone, "Toward a Fourth Generation of Revolutionary Theory," *Annual Review of Political Science* 4 (2001): 141–2.

11 Goldstone, "Toward a Fourth Generation," 175.

12 Jack Goldstone, "Theory Development in the Study of Revolutions," *New Directions in Contemporary Sociological Theory*, ed. Joseph Berger and Morris Zelditch, Jr. (Lanham, MD: Rowman & Littlefield, 2002), 222.

THE EVOLVING DEBATE

KEY POINTS

- Although the Iranian Revolution* of 1979 did not conform to Skocpol's theory, she modified her theory in response to it, emphasizing narratives of resistance in the Shia* branch of Islam and the role of abusive dictatorships.

- The social scientist Timothy Wickham-Crowley* advanced Skocpol's project by analyzing Latin American cases in the twentieth century.

- The sociologist* Jack Goldstone* advances this concept further to encompass the Arab Uprisings* that began in 2010, often known as the "Arab Spring."

Uses and Problems

The key factor moving the debate forward between Theda Skocpol (representing the more comparative* approaches to understanding revolution drawn in *States and Social Revolutions*, in which structural factors at the level of the state were important) and dissenters from what we may think of as the orthodoxy she established was not agreement but, rather, changing circumstances.

The Iranian Revolution, the Nicaraguan Revolution,* and revolutions throughout the world following the end of the colonial period, have challenged scholars to "broaden their scope of comparative studies beyond the classical revolutions of Europe."[1] This is because Iran showed that a middle-class, urban revolution fought in a state that experienced no external competition (in the vein of the revolutions she studied in 1979, at least) can still occur, and still reorder society "top to bottom."

> **❝**Revolutionary movements will undoubtedly continue to emerge in the Third World, where many states are not only exclusionary, but also fiscally, administratively, and militarily weak. And if the past is any guide, such movements will be especially likely to triumph where the political regimes they oppose remain narrow as well as repressive. **❞**
>
> Jeff Goodwin and Theda Skocpol, "Explaining Revolutions in the Contemporary Third World"

In a paper coauthored with the sociologist Jeff Goodwin,* Skocpol keeps many of her ideas about state autonomy and the principle that revolutions are the product of structural* forces consistent. Destitution in the developing world may be intense, but states with high rates of poverty do not always experience revolutions: "multiparty democracies or quasi democracies" do not tend to experience revolutions, whereas "organizationally weak (or suddenly weakened) authoritarian* regimes" are more prone to experience uprising.[2] Regimes that are unable to reform their oppression ("strategies of rule characteristic of direct colonialism and … neo-patrimonial dictatorship") in the face of sudden weakness against internal revolutionary coalitions are vulnerable to revolution.[3] "Neo-patrimonial dictatorship" refers to a system in which the dictator distributes state resources to secure influence, loyalty, and the continuance of the system itself. Much like the agrarian* autocracies* of France, China, and Russia, patrimonial* dictatorships (like prerevolutionary Iran) control vast swathes of their economy, often rewarding family and friends with control of entire industries and sacrifice efficiency for personal aggrandizement.[4]

Schools of Thought

In the 1980s and 1990s, *States and Social Revolutions* inspired other works of macro-comparative history (an approach to historical analysis that compares historical factors and phenomena on the large scale: over long periods, or at the level of nations). One scholar Skocpol cites in *Social Revolutions in the Modern World* as continuing the project particularly well is Timothy-Wickham Crowley, who extends the methodology to more recent revolutions in the modern world, and who remains in the third-generation tradition in his emphasis on social structures. He shares with Skocpol the conception of the state as an important actor, and state breakdown as the key factor in opening up the state for revolutionary change. Finally, he sees "revolution" as a more fixed category.

Wickham-Crowley uses Boolean algebra*—a method allowing analysis to be conducted according to logical principles—to examine the "necessary" and "sufficient" underlying causes of revolution, and to determine which configuration of causes leads to revolutionary change. This is a very distinctive method for attributing the cause of a given outcome to a number of underlying factors. It holds that there is not only one way for the outcome to come about, but many ways—and that no single factor can "cause" the outcome; all factors work together. "Each scenario that emerges," Wickham-Crowley writes of his methodology, "describes a structure of interrelated conditions, rather than a list of variables" to be controlled and measured.[5] This is called "qualitative comparative analysis."*

Wickham-Crowley thinks five underlying factors come together to cause revolution. Referencing irregular "guerrilla"* fighting forces, he argues: "Revolutionaries came to power in Latin America from 1956 to 1988 only when a rural-based guerrilla movement secured strong peasant support in the countryside and achieved military-level strength," and if the movement faced off against a "patrimonial" regime, in which a dictator distributed state resources to certain high-status individuals in order to secure cross-class or cross-region support, the dictatorship was disrupted (either through the withdrawal of support, or by pressure to bow to revolution).[6]

Wickham-Crowley's theory differs from Skocpol's in a number of key ways; notably, he is not interested in "world historical" revolutions (that is, revolutions that describe world trends associated with the transition to modernity) but in the brittleness of authoritarianism. In part, this is because Skocpol was analyzing the social revolutions involved in the transition of society to the modern age, while Wickham-Crowley's focus was the analysis of teetering authoritarian states—a distinctively modern phenomenon.

In Current Scholarship

Jack Goldstone is one key theorist of revolutionary change working today. His recent work has focused on assessing the causes of the Arab Uprisings that began in 2010 against authoritarian regimes that "appear unshakeable" but that "are actually highly vulnerable."[7] He suggests that, for a revolution to succeed (and become a "social revolution"), the military elite must be alienated from the state apparatus, a wide swath of people—multi-ethnic, multi-class—must mobilize, and international support must either withdraw (if it exists) or intervene to prevent the government from using the full force at its disposal (for example, chemical weapons, killing protestors, and so on). What is most important, however, is the failure of a "sultanistic"* regime (an order in which the dictator and his friends control the military, business, and foreign contact) to continue to hold up an authoritarian bargain.

In essence, the bargain is the purchasing of citizens' political apathy in exchange for distributing wealth. So the external threat, in this case, is spiking food prices and unemployment, undermining the authoritarian bargain. Like Skocpol, Goldstone argues (though more circumspectly), that underlying conditions combine with external issues to prompt popular uprising in the face of state weakening.

NOTES

1   Jeff Goodwin and Theda Skocpol, "Explaining Revolutions in the Contemporary Third World," *Politics and Society* 17, no. 4 (1989): 489.

2   Goodwin and Skocpol, "Explaining Revolutions," 495.

3   Goodwin and Skocpol, "Explaining Revolutions," 505.

4   Goodwin and Skocpol, "Explaining Revolutions," 499.

5   Timothy Wickham-Crowley, "A Qualitative Comparative Approach to Latin American Revolutions," *International Journal of Comparative Sociology* 32, 1–2 (1991): 103.

6   Wickham-Crowley, "A Qualitative Comparative Approach to Latin American Revolutions," 99.

7   Jack Goldstone, "Understanding the Revolutions of 2011: Weakness and Resilience in Middle Eastern Autocracies," *Foreign Affairs* 90, no. 3 (2011): 8.

IMPACT AND INFLUENCE TODAY

KEY POINTS

- *States and Social Revolutions* is a book emblematic of a structural way of thinking; its successors (rather than the book itself) remain academically relevant.

- The scholars Eric Selbin* and Charles Tilly* suggest that agency*—especially narratives of resistance, and conflict over who "owns" the narrative—forms an important part of revolutionary conflict, and is relevant to an analysis of revolution.

- The international relations* scholar George Lawson* does not necessarily argue against them, but reasserts the importance of structure* in creating openings for "negotiated" revolutionary change.

Position

Today, Theda Skocpol's *States and Social Revolutions: A Comparative Analysis of France, Russia, and China* is more representative of a particular position in the debate on the roots of revolution rather than an "active" participant. The sociologist John Foran* writes: "Ever since Theda Skocpol's pathbreaking study … structural theories have been the approach of choice, whether taking off from or criticizing her work."[1] Her work is important to both "sides" in the debate because, in recent years, the basis of the debate (structure versus agency) is no longer at the center of current scholarship. Instead, scholarship has been focused on integrating these two positions. "Suffice it to say," writes Timothy Wickham-Crowley,* "reports of the death of 'structural theorizing' about revolution … are greatly exaggerated," and Skocpol serves as an example of the

> **❝** In the modern era, revolutions have been seen as festivals of violence, fights to the finish in which one side vanquishes the other, an ultimate victory in which a new order is instituted while the ashes of the old are still burning ... Negotiated revolutions offer a radically different conceptualization of violence than past examples of revolution. Negotiated transformations are not violent fights to the finish but relatively peaceful processes in which deals are struck between revolutionaries and their adversaries. **❞**
>
> George Lawson, *Negotiated Revolutions*

enduring power of this method.[2] Ultimately, the fourth generation* of revolutionary scholarship encouraged scholars to look at both sides of the question: How are actors constrained, and what do they choose to do with those constraints?

Since its publication in 1979, *States and Social Revolutions* has encouraged scholars either to develop the book's ideas (among them Timothy Wickham-Crowley and Jeff Goodwin*), or to take issue with them (among them Eric Selbin or Farideh Farhi*). Farhi, for example, in the aftermath of the Iranian Revolution* (which appeared not to conform to Skocpol's theory) reinterprets some of Skocpol's key conclusions in light of this fact. She relocates Skocpol's theory in terms of (among other things) resistance to capitalist* expansion around the world.[3] Generally, though, *States and Social Revolutions* is cited at the beginning of books as representative of the structuralist position, and for its definition of revolution as total, bottom-up change.

Interaction

While there may be several structural, state-centric approaches to revolution, the debate about the extent to which agency plays a role in the formulation grows. Because of the importance of symbolism, collective memory, and "the social context of politics," writes Eric Selbin, "ideas and actors, not structures and some broad sweep of history, are the primary forces in revolutionary processes."[4] Selbin suggests differing populations have differing "revolutionary potential," offering a "perception of the options that are available and seem plausible to them," or "repertoires of collective action"—the shared belief in the Shia* branch of Islam, for example, according to which resistance to unjust power is a quasi-religious duty.[5]

Why does Selbin restate the importance of agency in the face of the relatively strong argument for structure? It is because structural conditions (which constrain options available to people) and social outcomes (which are the things we try to predict) are mediated by people's actions, and people have many different things they can do with the same set of social conditions. Revolutionary conflict, then, is not just a conflict of resources and control over state apparatus, but also "contention and confrontation over symbols" between revolutionary leaders and those in power.[6]

Charles Tilly gives an example of how this may play out. The Zapatistas,* a revolutionary group in Mexico, writes Tilly, "through the mouth, pen, and [radio transmitter]," declared themselves "to be the local manifestation of a popular movement extending back to the Spanish Conquest" of South America starting in the fifteenth century.[7] They project themselves as continuing a struggle against unjust, corrupt power: "Their identity resides not in the sum of their common attributes ... but in their collective relation to Mexican power" and Mexican liberation.[8]

The Continuing Debate

It is a mistake to think of fourth-generation scholars of revolution as either "structure" thinkers *or* "agency" thinkers; they are, rather, scholars who are more interested in studying states and international developments, and the ways in which actors are constrained; other scholars (like Selbin and Tilly) are interested in what potential revolutionaries do with those constraints.

One example of a scholar moving the structural side of the discipline forward is George Lawson, author of the book *Negotiated Revolutions* (2004). Lawson appeals to the changes in the Czech Republic, South Africa, and Chile, where successful revolutions occurred without completely destabilizing the state. Lawson's theory suggests that, instead of trying to find utopia* (an ideal, unattainably perfect nation), negotiated revolutions seek liberation from tyranny, and to "catch up" with the liberal* international system.[9] Instead of waiting for the state to become weak and knocking it aside violently, revolutionaries and the state come to the negotiating table from a place of mutual weakness. This is usually connected to a shock felt by the regime internationally: for example, the withdrawal of the Soviet* security guarantee to the Czech Republic after the breakdown of the Warsaw Pact* in 1989 (the Warsaw Pact nations were Europe's communist* states). This is, actually, an important way in which agency "comes in" to negotiated revolutionary theory: even though the revolutionary situation is created by structural forces abroad, "revolutions are a complex interplay between changing structural conditions and collective action," where actors can *choose* "roundtables rather than guillotines."[10] And finally, because negotiated revolutions aim at liberation rather than utopia, they result in smaller, less bureaucratic, states.

NOTES

1   John Foran, "Introduction," in *Theorizing Revolutions*, ed. John Foran (London: Routledge, 1997), 2.

2   Timothy Wickham-Crowley, "Structural Theories of Revolution," in *Theorizing Revolutions*, ed. John Foran (London: Routledge, 1997), 61.

3   Farideh Farhi, "State Disintegration and Urban-Based Revolutionary Crisis: A Comparative Analysis of Iran and Nicaragua," *Comparative Political Studies* 21, no. 2 (1988): 231.

4   Eric Selbin, "Revolution in the Real World: Bringing Agency Back In," in *Theorizing Revolutions*, ed. John Foran (London: Routledge, 1997), 123.

5   Selbin, "Revolution in the Real World," 125.

6   Selbin, "Revolution in the Real World," 130.

7   Charles Tilly, *Stories, Identities, and Political Change* (Lanham, MD: Rowman & Littlefield, 2002), 7.

8   Tilly, *Stories, Identities, and Political Change*, 9.

9   George Lawson, *Negotiated Revolutions: The Czech Republic, South Africa, and Chile,* (Aldershot: Ashgate, 2005), 227.

10   Lawson, *Negotiated Revolutions*, 232.

MODULE 12
WHERE NEXT?

KEY POINTS

- The notion of the specific causes of revolution has changed as globalization* (increasing political, cultural, and economic ties across continental borders) and technological development create new grievances and forms of association.

- The international relations* scholar George Lawson* turns to the Arab Uprisings* to understand the extent to which "sultanistic"* states can prevent revolution.

- Theda Skocpol's *States and Social Revolution* helped define the way a generation of scholars thought about revolution, pointing especially to the international and the state.

Potential

Theda Skocpol's *States and Social Revolutions: A Comparative Analysis of France, Russia, and China* is a highly important work, serving as the archetype of third-generation theories of revolution* in its emphasis on structural* factors such as class and the nature of the economy. However, as Skocpol herself noted, "scholarly works in the social sciences start to become outdated the moment they are published," as new forms of revolution (from the "negotiated" revolutions of the post-communist* era, to the populist, urban uprisings in the Arab world) take root globally.[1]

The sociologist* John Foran,* in his edited volume *The Future of Revolutions*, writes that "two themes in the globalization literature" may become pertinent to the examination of revolutions in the future: "the debate on the extent of world poverty, and the thesis on the declining significance of the nation-state.*"[2] That is, people are doing

72

> **❝** The twentieth century we depart appears in many ways the classic age of revolutions, in Theda Skocpol's sense ... As we now enter the headlong era of globalization, the future of revolutions is ... more mass movements for social justice. **❞**
>
> John Foran, "Introduction," *The Future of Revolutions*

worse and worse, and the ability of the nation state to remedy this state of affairs is limited (in the face of transnational corporations, transnational terrorist organizations, and international institutions)— or so the theory goes.

Is it direct competition with other states that brings revolution, or is it "lagging behind" a global system? The cultural critic Douglas Kellner* points out, further, how solidarity is no longer confined to autonomous peasants in agrarian* autocracies,* but that information and plans can be "instantly communicated to large numbers of individuals throughout the world."[3] So, many of the specific dynamics Skocpol highlights may no longer be relevant, while some of her key insights (that the state is not simply the puppet of class interests, or that the pressure causing revolution is more likely to be international in character) continue to inform study.

Future Directions

Revolutions continue to be a distinctive feature of world politics, and their study (especially in light of the Arab Uprisings that began in 2010) remains of crucial importance. George Lawson, a more recent theorist of revolutions, has recently written about how we might be able to theorize the Arab Uprisings. "International dynamics," he argues, "were the precipitant cause," meaning they provided the underlying kindling waiting for the revolutionary spark; outcomes of the revolution were (in part) determined by the level of elite control over military and police forces; and, finally, information technologies (such as Twitter and Facebook) may have raised participation, but did not in themselves "engender major transformations."[4]

Lawson points to international forces as not only working to stir up revolution, but also to "decompress" revolution. "Repression, aid, and sectarian polarization" was the strategy of the Gulf monarchies;* the distribution of massive financial packages to either states or non-state groups in the region meant either protests were stopped before they could start (as was the case in Morocco, where a combination of constitutional reform and the distribution of money headed revolutionary sentiment off at the pass), or they descended into sectarian violence (as was the case in Libya and Syria).[5]

Summary

Theda Skocpol's *States and Social Revolutions*, in summary, presented a vision of revolution—total change of every relationship, political and social, within a state—that suggested revolutions are not "made" by angry or idealistic revolutionaries, but rather, they "come" as agrarian bureaucracies* lose their grips on their states.

As time went on, however, revolutions in the real world (such as those in Iran*) seemed to run counter to the theory: an ideologically driven urban revolt against a state that did not face major competition from outside is nearly opposite to what Skocpol would expect. Skocpol, however, was not intending to make a universal theory of all revolutions forever, but rather a specific type of "modernizing"* revolution, bound up with the spread of industrialization and capitalism* around the world. Inheritors of Skocpol's project were more interested in late-twentieth and twenty-first-century style revolutions, more concerned with guerrilla* war, transnational attempts at democratization, ideology, and nonviolence. Fourth-generation theories of revolution set aside the absolute polarity between approaches emphasizing agency ("revolutions are made by those who decide to revolt") and those emphasizing structure ("revolutions arise when certain conditions come together"). More recent scholarship has suggested that revolutionaries *can* be enabled by structural conditions, but it is up to them to choose what to do with those conditions.

NOTES

1   Theda Skocpol, *Social Revolutions in the Modern World* (Cambridge: Cambridge University Press, 1994), 3.

2   John Foran, "Introduction to the Future of Revolutions," in *The Future of Revolutions: Rethinking Radical Change in the Age of Globalization*, ed. John Foran (London: Zed Books, 2003), 5.

3   Douglas Kellner, "Globalization, Technopolitics, and Revolution," in *The Future of Revolutions: Rethinking Radical Change in the Age of Globalization*, ed. John Foran (London: Zed Books, 2003), 182.

4   George Lawson, "Revolution, Non-violence, and the Arab Uprisings," *Mobilization: An International Quarterly*, August 2015, accessed November 1, 2015, http://eprints.lse.ac.uk/63156/1/Lawson_Revolution%2C%20non-violence.pdf, 3.

5   Lawson, "Revolution, Non-violence, and the Arab Uprisings," 21.

GLOSSARY

GLOSSARY OF TERMS

Agency: individual motivations and volition; analytical approaches focusing on agency look at the ways in which people make their own choices and act independently of outside forces.

Agrarian: a mode of life centered on farming; an agrarian economy is based primarily on agricultural production.

American Civil War (1861–65): a war in the United States fought between the "Union" Northern states and the "Confederate" Southern states, which had attempted to secede from the United States over several contentious issues, largely pertaining to slavery, states' rights, and similar. The war ended with a Union victory.

American Political Science Association: an American professional association of academics, founded in 1903, in the field of political science.

Apartheid (1948–94): an Afrikaans word meaning "apartness," this was the official racial policy of South Africa, where black people were provided with inferior (or no) public services, and in many cases stripped of citizenship. The policy led to a long-standing embargo of the state as well as internal resistance.

Arab Uprisings: a series of political uprisings that occurred in the Arab world between 2010 and 2013, starting with the self-immolation of a fruit vendor in Tunisia. Mostly, they have not resulted in sustained political change, and have contributed to growing instability in the region.

Authoritarianism: a system of rule in which one group or person rules for an indefinite period of time, and within which dissent is not tolerated.

Autocracy: a system of rule in which power is held by a single person.

Bolsheviks: a Russian political action group primarily comprising urban workers, who would play a major role in the 1917 Revolution and go on to form the majority of the government of the Soviet Union in 1922.

Boolean algebra: a method in logic. Instead of representing numbers, however, variables represent "true" or "false." The main operations of Boolean algebra are conjunction (and), disjunction (or), and negation (not).

Bourbon monarchy: the French family that between 1589 and 1848 ruled a number of territories throughout Europe, at their greatest extent controlling Spain, Naples, Sicily, Parma, much of Spain, and Luxembourg. The dynasty saw Louis XIV, one of the most powerful rulers in French history, aggressively centralize and bureaucratize the state. His descendant, Louis XVI, fell victim to the French Revolution and was executed in Paris in 1793.

Bourgeoisie: a social class; formally the people who came to own factories during the industrial revolution, but commonly used to refer to the middle and upper-middle classes.

Bureaucracy: a term referring to the power of appointed technical experts in government, acting in an administrative capacity as government staff rather than governors.

Capitalism: a social and economic system in which the resources required for production are held in private hands, with the goal of selling on production to make profit in a market economy.

Case selection: a step in the research process, whereby the researcher chooses the cases (individual instances of an event, people, and so on) to be studied.

Causal inference: the process of drawing a connection between a prior event (a cause) and a subsequent event (an effect), where if it were not for the cause, the effect would not have happened.

Chinese Revolution: the conflict that occurred between the Chinese Communist Party (formed 1921) and the Kuomintang, or Chinese Nationalist Party. China was officially declared communist in 1949, and Mao Zedong assumed chairmanship of the state until his death in 1976.

Civil Rights Movement: the term used to refer to a number of related social movements in the United States from the 1950s in order to demand equality for African Americans.

Cold War: a period (1947–91) of tension between the United States and the Soviet Union and the nations aligned to them. While the two blocs never engaged in direct military conflict, they engaged in covert and proxy wars and espionage against one another.

Communism: a socioeconomic system based on the shared ownership of the means of production (the resources and tools required for manufacturing, for example) by a community.

Comparative method: a method of analysis that involves examining two cases and identifying the underlying factors that have driven their respective outcomes.

Complexity: a "complex" system contains many parts, which interact with each other in mutually interdependent and unpredictable ways, and often have emergent properties.

Containment: a policy implemented during the Cold War based on active work by the United States to prevent the spread of communism.

Decolonization: the process by which European states relinquished foreign possessions accumulated under the auspices of their empire; this process occurred primarily during the latter half of the twentieth century.

Deduction: the logical practice of taking an absolutely true major premise ("All men are mortal"), an absolutely true minor premise ("Socrates is a man"), and coming to an absolutely true conclusion ("Socrates is mortal").

Dependent variable: when examining the effect of one thing on another thing (the effect of arm strength on the distance an apple is thrown, for example), the former is the "independent variable" (the thing causing the effect) and the latter is the "dependent variable" (the thing effected by the cause).

Empiricism: a theory of knowledge that holds that knowledge comes only from what one can observe.

Fascism: a system of far right-wing government that emphasizes nationalism (often to the point of extreme racism) and military strength (often to the point of aggression), and involves a single dictator having extreme power related to enforcing order and national unity. Nazi Germany is a classic example of a fascist state.

Federalism: a system of government in which administrative power is shared between different levels of government (Germany, for example, has both a national government and state governments).

Fourth-generation revolutionary theory: a trend in revolutionary theory that, while poorly defined compared with previous generations, sees stability as its outcome of interest, and looks at combinations of structural factors and agent factors.

French Revolution: a decade of intense political upheaval in France (1789–99), in which the revolutionaries experimented with a variety of different regimes, including a constitutional monarchy, a revolutionary dictatorship, a popular direct democracy and a liberal republic, before ending with the military dictatorship of Napoleon Bonaparte.

Globalization: the process of increasing interconnectedness around the globe, driven by improvements in travel, shipping, and telecommunications among other technologies.

Grand theory: an abstract theory meant to explain a wide swathe of behavior with reference to one thing.

Guerrilla: Spanish term meaning "little war," a "guerrilla war" occurs when a small group fights a much larger, stronger foe, by remaining invisible and mobile, striking at enemies where they are weak (such as attacking supply chains) or only focusing on important targets (such as conducting assassinations).

Gulf monarchies: states in the Persian (also called Arabian) Gulf, ruled by Sunni kings and aristocracies, depending (primarily) on oil revenue. They include Kuwait, Bahrain, the United Arab Emirates, Saudi Arabia, Qatar, and Oman.

Historical materialism: an approach to social sciences (first put forward by the German economist and philosopher Karl Marx) that asserts that the economic underpinnings of a society (rather than, say, choices made by leaders, ideology, and so on) define how the social structures emerge and are the principle drivers of historical events.

Ideology: a comprehensive political and social vision of how life ought to be, relating to the goals, expectations, and motivations of entire groups of people (and may also extend to beliefs about what those goals, expectations, and motivations should be for others as well). It is a system of thought, extended to the practical.

Induction: a logical operation, comparable to deduction. Instead of presenting absolutely true premises, however (which do not occur often in real life, or when they do occur are not particularly useful), induction aims at presenting the probably true. An example of inductive reasoning is: "People with large boats are often happy," "People with large boats often have a lot of money," so "Money probably helps make people happy."

Industrialization: the process by which a country or region adopts a primarily industrial economy, at the expense of a primarily agricultural economy.

International institution: in international relations, an international institution refers to a set of principles, norms, and decision-making procedures agreed by a number of actors who explicitly or implicitly agree to abide by them. Examples include the United Nations, the International Monetary Fund, and the World Trade Organization.

International relations: the branch of political science that studies the interactions between states and foreign policies.

Iranian Revolution: the overthrow of the Western-backed Shah of Iran in 1979, instituting its present-day Islamic Republic. The revolution featured urban strikes that damaged the state economy combined with mass protests. Ayatollah Ruhollah Khomeini was its leader in exile, who combined anti-Western, anti-Shah sentiment with Islamic theology.

Jacobinism: a political movement of the French Revolution that championed radical left-wing ideology, state centralization, and the elimination of perceived enemies of the revolution at all costs.

Liberalism: a political philosophy that emphasizes individual choice and freedom.

Marxism: an approach to social sciences (and humanities) rooted in the philosophy of the nineteenth-century German political philosopher Karl Marx. It holds that dialectics (meaning two opposing forces) define history, and those dialectics are rooted in class. Ultimately, it holds that everything else, such as religion, politics, art, and so on, flows from this class relationship (whereby one group controls the means of production and exploits another).

Marxist-Leninism: an adaptation of Marxism by the Russian revolutionary leader Vladimir Lenin, where the way to institute a classless, utopian society is through a revolution that would bring one-party rule to the state, force collectivization of all industry, and export the revolution globally.

Means of production: a concept in Marxism; the material through which the main mode of production is carried out. In feudalism, this is control of land for agricultural production; in capitalism, this is control of factories for industrial production.

Meiji Restoration: the formal hand-over of power in Japan in 1868 from feudal warlords called *Daimyo* led by a *Shogun* to a strong, centralized imperial government. The restoration aimed to modernize and standardize Japan's economy, in order to compete with European/ Western nations that had previously forced Japan to sign nonadvantageous treaties.

Modernization: the process by which a state discards traditional economic and social practices and technologies, and adopts modern equivalents.

Monarchy: a form of government in which sovereignty is imbued in one person for their lifetime, and legitimacy is commonly based on descent. Even in elected monarchies, only people of a certain lineage are able to vote.

Nation state: a political entity whose legitimacy derives from its status as encompassing a whole "cultural" group (for example, people sharing language, religion, and shared identity).

Nicaraguan Revolution: an uprising in the Latin American nation of Nicaragua in 1979 by left-leaning Sandinista rebels, using guerrilla tactics (kidnapping, jungle warfare, and so on) against the corrupt (but US-backed) Somoza regime.

Patrimonialism: a form of government in which all power flows from the leader, and politics tends to be structured around gaining the patronage of the leader.

Practicum: a style of class, often undertaken by graduate students, that involves the practical application of some studied theory or practice.

Prussian Revolution: an uprising in 1848, based primarily in Berlin, against King Frederick William IV, which initially held to liberal principles, but was co-opted by the aristocracy. This was one of several revolutions that occurred in central Europe, France, and Italy that year.

Qualitative comparative analysis: a research method, consisting of both an approach to data and a method of analysis. The fundamentals of this approach are similar to the comparative method, where mostly different cases that lead to the same outcomes, or vice versa, are analyzed for the key factors driving outcomes.

Rational choice theory: a framework for modeling behavior, where it is assumed that agents are self-regarding (meaning they look out for their own interests) utility maximizers (meaning they aim to increase their own welfare as much as possible). The framework came into doubt, however, when it became increasingly clear that people are more prone to make bad decisions on the basis of limited information.

Rationalization: the process of implementing "means–ends" rationality in more segments of society (that is, changing the way things are done to make them more efficient, predictable, and impersonal).

Republic: a form of government in which citizens elect representatives in order to govern for them, and where the representatives are accountable to the citizens.

Research program: a concept in the philosophy of science, describing how a given paradigm gives rise to scientific advancement. A research program contains a "hard-core" assumption (which cannot change, or else the research program will end), from which flow "malleable theories" (which can change based on empirical evidence).

Russian Revolution: an uprising in 1917 against the autocratic government of the monarch Tsar Nicolas II that occurred in the midst of heavy Russian losses in World War I. The revolution led to the establishment of a communist government in Russia, and, in 1922, the formation of the Soviet Union.

Shia Islam: the second largest sect of Islam (after the Sunni branch) that disagrees with the majority on which family line properly succeeded the Prophet Mohammed. Doctrinal differences between the two sects include, but are certainly not limited to, the uniquely Shi'a belief that clerics can continue to update and reinterpret holy texts.

Social policy: the set of policy instruments concerned with addressing collectively defined problems, often associated with promotion of welfare for citizens.

Social revolution: a "total" revolution, whereby all the economic, social, and political relationships in a given country are changed entirely.

Sovereignty: the control of a body (usually a state) over defined territory and citizens, exclusive of all other claims to control those areas (for example, the United States has sovereign control over the country that is the USA, and its citizens, and Canada does not, and vice versa).

Soviet Union: also known as the USSR, a kind of "super state" that existed from 1922 to 1991, centered primarily on Russia and its neighbors in Eastern Europe and the northern half of Asia. It was the communist pole of the Cold War, with the United States as its main "rival."

Structure: regularities and rules in social interactions; analytical approaches focusing on structure look at the ways in which people react predictably to consistent limits on their options.

Sultanism: a form of government characterized by the personal involvement of the leader in all forms of life; the permission of the sultan is required for any social, economic, or political movement to exist.

Third-generation revolutionary theory: a fashion in theorizing revolutions most exemplified by *States and Social Revolutions*. It sees its outcome of interest as whether or not there is a revolution, and emphasizes the role of structural factors.

Totalitarianism: a form of government characterized by the extreme priority and power of the state in all aspects of daily life, especially attempting to control the thoughts of its subjects. The difference between authoritarianism and totalitarianism is that the former is more concerned with citizens' actions rather than what they believe, whereas the latter is concerned with everything.

Tsar: the title given to the ruler of Russia (and its empire) from 1547 to 1917.

Utopia: a paradise, or otherwise perfect situation. The term also means a kind of impossibly perfect place.

Viet Cong: the popular name given to the Vietnamese National Liberation Front (NLF) that was aligned with the communist cause during the Vietnam War; representatives of North Vietnam. Using Soviet support, its guerrilla tactics helped force the United States to withdraw from Vietnam in 1973 and defeat its South Vietnamese allies in 1975.

Vietnam War: a two-decade-long military conflict between communist forces, led by North Vietnam, and anti-communist forces, led by the United States and South Vietnam. Starting in 1955 and finishing in 1975 following the withdrawal of American troops from Vietnamese territory, this was the longest sustained conflict with direct US military involvement during the Cold War.

Warsaw Pact: a mutual defense and cooperation agreement between the communist states of Europe during the Cold War from 1955 to 1991, whereby any security threat (from within or without) would be countered by the extremely powerful Soviet military. The dissolution of this pact led to widespread uprisings throughout Eastern Europe.

Welfare state: a concept in government whereby the state is conceived as providing for the welfare (well-being) of its citizens, usually through transfers of funds from some individuals, via the state, to others in the form of healthcare, social care, or even direct transfers.

World-systems theory: an approach to world sociology and history that turns on the idea that some countries are systematically exploited by others.

Zapatista Army of National Liberation: a left-wing revolutionary group in southern Mexico, associated with indigenous Maya people of the region.

PEOPLE MENTIONED IN THE TEXT

Daniel Bell (1919–2011) was an American sociologist, most notable for his work on the nature of the post-industrial world, and the exhaustion of grand ideology in modernity.

Michael Burawoy (b. 1947) is a British sociologist and Marxist currently at the University of California at Berkeley.

Émile Durkheim (1858–1917) was a French sociologist, and is considered one of the founders of the discipline. His book *Suicide*, published in 1897, is concerned with the interaction of social institutions, modernity, and the ways in which they shape choice.

Peter B. Evans (b. 1944) is an American international sociologist at the University of California at Berkeley. His work addresses the evolving relationship between state and society in the context of globalization.

Farideh Farhi (b. 1955) is an American Iranian academic affiliated with the University of Hawaii, who, in addition to academic work on revolutions in the developing world, has also worked with such institutions as the World Bank.

John Foran (b. 1955) is an American sociologist at the University of California, Santa Barbara. His interests include justice, radicalism, and the culture of the developing world.

Barbara Geddes is an American sociologist at the University of California at Los Angeles. Her work, focusing on Latin America, looks at the breakdown of authoritarian regimes.

Jack Goldstone (b. 1953) is an American sociologist who studies the intersection of social movements and global politics, especially in early modern Europe. He is the author of *Revolution and Rebellion in the Early Modern World* (1991).

Jeff Goodwin (b. 1958) is a comparative historical sociologist at New York University.

Ted Gurr (b. 1936) is an American sociologist at the University of Nevada, Las Vegas, and his work (including *Why Men Rebel,* 1970) focuses on the role of deprivation in enraging people into rebelling.

Michael Hechter (b. 1943) is a professor of sociology at the University of Washington. His work focuses on how to measure individual values, especially in the context of nationalism.

G. W. F. Hegel (1770–1831) was a German philosopher and phenomenologist. His work, especially through his "Lectures on the Philosophy of History," delivered in Berlin during the 1820s, argued that "history" has a single logic of increasing human freedom, as the "ideal" of the mind asserts itself more and more on the real world, and slaves overthrow their masters. History, he believes, proceeds through conflict between contradictory forces, until human existence is perfected.

George C. Homans (1910–89) was an American sociologist, important in the behavioral tradition. This holds, jointly, that the basic principles of "the social" are common to all humans, and social life may be generalized from these basic principles. In 1950, he wrote *The Human Group*, which is still studied.

Chalmers Johnson (1931–2010) was an American political thinker and statesman, prominent during the Cold War, and author of *Revolutionary Change* (1966). He is famous for his theory that America's foreign-policy agenda makes it akin to a modern empire.

Douglas Kellner (b. 1943) is an academic in the tradition of critical theory. His work is concerned with ways in which people resist and embrace through new forms of media (called "technopolitics").

George F. Kennan (1904–2005) was an American statesman and international relations theorist. In 1946, he formulated the policy of "containment" designed to counter the foreign-policy objectives of the Soviet Union. He served as ambassador to the Soviet Union from 1951 to 1952. His 1947 article "The Sources of Soviet Conduct," for which he was credited only as "X," was among the most important of the Cold War.

George Lawson is an associate professor at the London School of Economics. He specializes in the history of international relations theory, and the idea of "the international."

Vladimir Lenin (1870–1924) was a Russian revolutionary, radical political thinker, and government figure. After leading the Russian Revolution in 1917, he became the first head of the one-party state in the Soviet Union, and helped set its mission of international expansion.

Seymour Martin Lipset (1922–2006) was an American sociologist and political advisor. His 1959 article "Some Social Requisites of Democracy" is considered seminal in the study of democratization.

Karl Marx (1818–83) was a German philosopher and social theorist. Initially a follower of Hegel, Marx believed that human society progresses through class struggle, and that capitalism would give way to socialism. *Capital* (1867–83 over several volumes) and *The Communist Manifesto* (1848) both helped inspire revolutions in politics and scholarship.

John Stuart Mill (1806–73) was an English philosopher, economist, and politician. He was concerned with understanding ways in which individuals could justify their liberty on a rational basis. His 1843 book *A System of Logic* laid out the comparative approach to causation.

C. Wright Mills (1916–62) was an American sociologist at Columbia University, whose book *The Sociological Imagination* (1959) specified how sociologists should see the world as an interplay between individual lives and broader histories.

Barrington Moore (1913–2005) was an American political scientist and a major figure in the comparative method and the sociology of instability. *Social Origins of Dictatorship and Democracy* (1966) is among his most prominent works.

Napoleon Bonaparte (1769–1821) was a French statesman and general, and creator of the French Empire, which lasted from 1804 to 1815 and dominated much of continental Europe.

Nicholas II (1868–1918) was the last tsar of the Russian empire. He was deposed by the Bolsheviks in 1917, and executed along with his family in 1918.

Mohammad Reza Shah Pahlavi (1919–80) was the Shah (king) of Iran from 1941 to 1979, when he was overthrown by the Islamic revolution. His reign was considered personalist and overly repressive, but friendly to Western interests.

Talcott Parsons (1902–79) was an American sociologist at Harvard University. His 1937 book *The Structure of Social Action* is considered seminal in the discipline.

Dietrich Rueschemeyer (b. 1930) is a German professor emeritus of sociology at Brown University in the United States.

Eric Selbin is an American sociologist of resistance and revolution, especially on the role of stories in fostering revolution.

William H. Sewell Jr. (b. 1940) is the Frank P. Hixon Distinguished Service Professor Emeritus of history and political science at the University of Chicago. He specializes in modern French social and cultural history; labor history; and social theory.

Charles Tilly (1929–2008) was an American political sociologist specializing in "contentious politics": the use of disruption to make a political change (especially in his *From Mobilization to Revolution* of 1978).

Leon Trotsky (1879–1940) was a Russian Marxist revolutionary and key leader in the Russian Revolution. He was excluded from government after Lenin's death by dictator Joseph Stalin, and lived in exile before being killed in Mexico.

Stephen Walt (b. 1955) is an American professor of international relations at Harvard University. He is associated with the realist tradition, which holds that conflict, rather than cooperation, characterizes world affairs. Among his more prominent books is *Revolution and War* (1996).

Max Weber (1864–1920) was a German sociologist, and is considered one of the founders of the discipline. He is a champion of interpretive sociology, whereby one analyses the meaning that people attach to their actions. Among his most famous books is *The Protestant Ethic and the Spirit of Capitalism* (1905).

Timothy Wickham-Crowley (b. 1951) is professor of sociology at Georgetown University in the United States. He is a specialist in Latin American revolutions, and for his 1992 book *Guerillas and Revolution in Latin America: A Comparative Study of Insurgents and Regimes since 1956.*

WORKS CITED

WORKS CITED

Burawoy, Michael. "Two Methods in Search of Science: Skocpol versus Trotsky." *Theory and Society* 18, no. 6 (1989): 759–805.

Durkheim, Émile. *Suicide: A Study in Sociology*. Edited by George Simpson. Translated by John A. Spaulding and George Simpson. London: Routledge, 2002.

Farhi, Farideh. "State Disintegration and Urban-Based Revolutionary Crisis: A Comparative Analysis of Iran and Nicaragua." *Comparative Political Studies* 21, no. 2 (1988): 231–56.

Foran, John. "Introduction." In *Theorizing Revolutions*, edited by John Foran, 1–8. London: Routledge, 1997.

"Introduction to the Future of Revolutions." In *The Future of Revolutions: Rethinking Radical Change in the Age of Globalization*, edited by John Foran, 1–17. London: Zed Books, 2003.

Geddes, Barbara. "How the Cases You Choose Affect the Answers You Get: Selection Bias in Comparative Politics." *Political Analysis* 2, no. 1 (1990): 131–50.

Goldstone, Jack A. "Theory Development in the Study of Revolutions." In *New Directions in Contemporary Sociological Theory,* edited by Joseph Berger and Morris Zelditch Jr., 194–226. Lanham, MD: Rowman & Littlefield, 2002.

"Toward a Fourth Generation of Revolutionary Theory." *Annual Review of Political Science* 4 (2001): 139–87.

Goodwin, Jeff. "Review: How to Become a Dominant American Social Scientist: The Case of Theda Skocpol." *Contemporary Sociology* 25, no. 3 (1996): 293–5.

"Understanding the Revolutions of 2011: Weakness and Resilience in Middle Eastern Autocracies." *Foreign Affairs* 90, no. 3 (2011): 8–16.

Goodwin, Jeff and Theda Skocpol. "Explaining Revolutions in the Contemporary Third World." *Politics and Society* 17, no. 4 (1989): 489–509.

Gurr, Ted. *Why Men Rebel.* Princeton, NJ: Princeton University Press, 1970.

Johnson, Chalmers. *Revolutionary Change.* Stanford, CA: Stanford University Press, 1982.

Kellner, Douglas. "Globalization, Technopolitics, and Revolution." In *The Future of Revolutions: Rethinking Radical Change in the Age of Globalization*, edited by John Foran, 180–94. London: Zed Books, 2003.

Lawson, George. *Negotiated Revolutions: The Czech Republic, South Africa, and Chile.* Aldershot: Ashgate, 2005.

"Revolution, Non-violence, and the Arab Uprisings." *Mobilization: An International Quarterly*. August 2015. Accessed November 1, 2015. http://eprints.lse.ac.uk/63156/1/Lawson_Revolution%2C%20non-violence.pdf.

Marx, Karl. *Early Writings*. Edited by Quentin Hoare. London: Penguin, 1975.

Mill, John Stuart. *A System of Logic: Volume I*. London: John W. Parker, 1851.

Mills, C. Wright. *The Sociological Imagination.* New York: Oxford University Press, 2000.

Moore, Barrington. *Social Origins of Dictatorship and Democracy*. London: Penguin, 1991.

Selbin, Eric. "Revolution in the Real World: Bringing Agency Back In." In *Theorizing Revolutions*, edited by John Foran, 118–32. London: Routledge, 1997.

Sewell Jr., William H. "Ideologies and Social Revolutions: Reflections on the French Case." *The Journal of Modern History* 57, no. 1 (1985): 57–85.

Skocpol, Theda. "Bringing the State Back In: Strategies of Analysis in Current Research." In *Bringing the State Back In*, edited by Peter B. Evans, Dietrich Rueschemeyer, and Theda Skocpol, 3–38. Cambridge: Cambridge University Press, 1985.

"Cultural Idioms and Political Ideologies in the Revolutionary Reconstruction of State Power: A Rejoinder to Sewell." *The Journal of Modern History* 57, no. 1 (1985): 86–96.

Interview by Richard Snyder, May 14, 2002. "Theda Skocpol: States, Revolutions, and the Comparative Historical Imagination". In *Passion, Craft, and Method in Comparative Politics*, edited by Geraldo J. Munck and Richard Snyder, 649–708. Baltimore, MD: Johns Hopkins University Press, 2007.

Protecting Soldiers and Mothers: The Political Origins of Social Policy in the United States. Cambridge, MA: Belknap Press, 1992.

"Rentier State and Shi'a Islam in the Iranian Revolution." *Theory and Society* 11, no. 3 (1982): 265–83.

States and Social Revolutions: A Comparative Analysis of France, Russia, and China. Cambridge: Cambridge University Press, 1979.

Tilly, Charles. *From Mobilization to Revolution*. Reading, MA: Addison Wesley, 1978.

Stories, Identities, and Political Change. Lanham, MD: Rowman & Littlefield, 2002.

Walt, Stephen. "Top Ten IR Books by Women." *Foreign Policy*, April 14, 2009. Accessed October 27, 2015. http://foreignpolicy.com/2009/04/14/top-ten-ir-books-by-women/?wp_login_redirect=0.

Weber, Max. *The Protestant Ethic and the Spirit of Capitalism*. New York: Scribner's, 1958.

Wickham-Crowley, Timothy. "A Qualitative Comparative Approach to Latin American Revolutions." *International Journal of Comparative Sociology* 32, no. 1–2 (1991): 82–109.

"Structural Theories of Revolution." In *Theorizing Revolutions*, edited by John Foran, 36–70. London: Routledge, 1997.

"X" [George F. Kennan]. "The Sources of Soviet Conduct." *Foreign Affairs* 65, no. 4 (1987): 852–68.

THE MACAT LIBRARY
BY DISCIPLINE

AFRICANA STUDIES

Chinua Achebe's *An Image of Africa: Racism in Conrad's Heart of Darkness*
W. E. B. Du Bois's *The Souls of Black Folk*
Zora Neale Huston's *Characteristics of Negro Expression*
Martin Luther King Jr's *Why We Can't Wait*
Toni Morrison's *Playing in the Dark: Whiteness in the American Literary Imagination*

ANTHROPOLOGY

Arjun Appadurai's *Modernity at Large: Cultural Dimensions of Globalisation*
Philippe Ariès's *Centuries of Childhood*
Franz Boas's *Race, Language and Culture*
Kim Chan & Renée Mauborgne's *Blue Ocean Strategy*
Jared Diamond's *Guns, Germs & Steel: the Fate of Human Societies*
Jared Diamond's *Collapse: How Societies Choose to Fail or Survive*
E. E. Evans-Pritchard's *Witchcraft, Oracles and Magic Among the Azande*
James Ferguson's *The Anti-Politics Machine*
Clifford Geertz's *The Interpretation of Cultures*
David Graeber's *Debt: the First 5000 Years*
Karen Ho's *Liquidated: An Ethnography of Wall Street*
Geert Hofstede's *Culture's Consequences: Comparing Values, Behaviors, Institutes and Organizations across Nations*
Claude Lévi-Strauss's *Structural Anthropology*
Jay Macleod's *Ain't No Makin' It: Aspirations and Attainment in a Low-Income Neighborhood*
Saba Mahmood's *The Politics of Piety: The Islamic Revival and the Feminist Subject*
Marcel Mauss's *The Gift*

BUSINESS

Jean Lave & Etienne Wenger's *Situated Learning*
Theodore Levitt's *Marketing Myopia*
Burton G. Malkiel's *A Random Walk Down Wall Street*
Douglas McGregor's *The Human Side of Enterprise*
Michael Porter's *Competitive Strategy: Creating and Sustaining Superior Performance*
John Kotter's *Leading Change*
C. K. Prahalad & Gary Hamel's *The Core Competence of the Corporation*

CRIMINOLOGY

Michelle Alexander's *The New Jim Crow: Mass Incarceration in the Age of Colorblindness*
Michael R. Gottfredson & Travis Hirschi's *A General Theory of Crime*
Richard Herrnstein & Charles A. Murray's *The Bell Curve: Intelligence and Class Structure in American Life*
Elizabeth Loftus's *Eyewitness Testimony*
Jay Macleod's *Ain't No Makin' It: Aspirations and Attainment in a Low-Income Neighborhood*
Philip Zimbardo's *The Lucifer Effect*

ECONOMICS

Janet Abu-Lughod's *Before European Hegemony*
Ha-Joon Chang's *Kicking Away the Ladder*
David Brion Davis's *The Problem of Slavery in the Age of Revolution*
Milton Friedman's *The Role of Monetary Policy*
Milton Friedman's *Capitalism and Freedom*
David Graeber's *Debt: the First 5000 Years*
Friedrich Hayek's *The Road to Serfdom*
Karen Ho's *Liquidated: An Ethnography of Wall Street*

The Macat Library By Discipline

John Maynard Keynes's *The General Theory of Employment, Interest and Money*
Charles P. Kindleberger's *Manias, Panics and Crashes*
Robert Lucas's *Why Doesn't Capital Flow from Rich to Poor Countries?*
Burton G. Malkiel's *A Random Walk Down Wall Street*
Thomas Robert Malthus's *An Essay on the Principle of Population*
Karl Marx's *Capital*
Thomas Piketty's *Capital in the Twenty-First Century*
Amartya Sen's *Development as Freedom*
Adam Smith's *The Wealth of Nations*
Nassim Nicholas Taleb's *The Black Swan: The Impact of the Highly Improbable*
Amos Tversky's & Daniel Kahneman's *Judgment under Uncertainty: Heuristics and Biases*
Mahbub Ul Haq's *Reflections on Human Development*
Max Weber's *The Protestant Ethic and the Spirit of Capitalism*

FEMINISM AND GENDER STUDIES

Judith Butler's *Gender Trouble*
Simone De Beauvoir's *The Second Sex*
Michel Foucault's *History of Sexuality*
Betty Friedan's *The Feminine Mystique*
Saba Mahmood's *The Politics of Piety: The Islamic Revival and the Feminist Subject*
Joan Wallach Scott's *Gender and the Politics of History*
Mary Wollstonecraft's *A Vindication of the Rights of Woman*
Virginia Woolf's *A Room of One's Own*

GEOGRAPHY

The Brundtland Report's *Our Common Future*
Rachel Carson's *Silent Spring*
Charles Darwin's *On the Origin of Species*
James Ferguson's *The Anti-Politics Machine*
Jane Jacobs's *The Death and Life of Great American Cities*
James Lovelock's *Gaia: A New Look at Life on Earth*
Amartya Sen's *Development as Freedom*
Mathis Wackernagel & William Rees's *Our Ecological Footprint*

HISTORY

Janet Abu-Lughod's *Before European Hegemony*
Benedict Anderson's *Imagined Communities*
Bernard Bailyn's *The Ideological Origins of the American Revolution*
Hanna Batatu's *The Old Social Classes And The Revolutionary Movements Of Iraq*
Christopher Browning's *Ordinary Men: Reserve Police Batallion 101 and the Final Solution in Poland*
Edmund Burke's *Reflections on the Revolution in France*
William Cronon's *Nature's Metropolis: Chicago And The Great West*
Alfred W. Crosby's *The Columbian Exchange*
Hamid Dabashi's *Iran: A People Interrupted*
David Brion Davis's *The Problem of Slavery in the Age of Revolution*
Nathalie Zemon Davis's *The Return of Martin Guerre*
Jared Diamond's *Guns, Germs & Steel: the Fate of Human Societies*
Frank Dikotter's *Mao's Great Famine*
John W Dower's *War Without Mercy: Race And Power In The Pacific War*
W. E. B. Du Bois's *The Souls of Black Folk*
Richard J. Evans's *In Defence of History*
Lucien Febvre's *The Problem of Unbelief in the 16th Century*
Sheila Fitzpatrick's *Everyday Stalinism*

Eric Foner's *Reconstruction: America's Unfinished Revolution, 1863-1877*
Michel Foucault's *Discipline and Punish*
Michel Foucault's *History of Sexuality*
Francis Fukuyama's *The End of History and the Last Man*
John Lewis Gaddis's *We Now Know: Rethinking Cold War History*
Ernest Gellner's *Nations and Nationalism*
Eugene Genovese's *Roll, Jordan, Roll: The World the Slaves Made*
Carlo Ginzburg's *The Night Battles*
Daniel Goldhagen's *Hitler's Willing Executioners*
Jack Goldstone's *Revolution and Rebellion in the Early Modern World*
Antonio Gramsci's *The Prison Notebooks*
Alexander Hamilton, John Jay & James Madison's *The Federalist Papers*
Christopher Hill's *The World Turned Upside Down*
Carole Hillenbrand's *The Crusades: Islamic Perspectives*
Thomas Hobbes's *Leviathan*
Eric Hobsbawm's *The Age Of Revolution*
John A. Hobson's *Imperialism: A Study*
Albert Hourani's *History of the Arab Peoples*
Samuel P. Huntington's *The Clash of Civilizations and the Remaking of World Order*
C. L. R. James's *The Black Jacobins*
Tony Judt's *Postwar: A History of Europe Since 1945*
Ernst Kantorowicz's *The King's Two Bodies: A Study in Medieval Political Theology*
Paul Kennedy's *The Rise and Fall of the Great Powers*
Ian Kershaw's *The "Hitler Myth": Image and Reality in the Third Reich*
John Maynard Keynes's *The General Theory of Employment, Interest and Money*
Charles P. Kindleberger's *Manias, Panics and Crashes*
Martin Luther King Jr's *Why We Can't Wait*
Henry Kissinger's *World Order: Reflections on the Character of Nations and the Course of History*
Thomas Kuhn's *The Structure of Scientific Revolutions*
Georges Lefebvre's *The Coming of the French Revolution*
John Locke's *Two Treatises of Government*
Niccolò Machiavelli's *The Prince*
Thomas Robert Malthus's *An Essay on the Principle of Population*
Mahmood Mamdani's *Citizen and Subject: Contemporary Africa And The Legacy Of Late Colonialism*
Karl Marx's *Capital*
Stanley Milgram's *Obedience to Authority*
John Stuart Mill's *On Liberty*
Thomas Paine's *Common Sense*
Thomas Paine's *Rights of Man*
Geoffrey Parker's *Global Crisis: War, Climate Change and Catastrophe in the Seventeenth Century*
Jonathan Riley-Smith's *The First Crusade and the Idea of Crusading*
Jean-Jacques Rousseau's *The Social Contract*
Joan Wallach Scott's *Gender and the Politics of History*
Theda Skocpol's *States and Social Revolutions*
Adam Smith's *The Wealth of Nations*
Timothy Snyder's *Bloodlands: Europe Between Hitler and Stalin*
Sun Tzu's *The Art of War*
Keith Thomas's *Religion and the Decline of Magic*
Thucydides's *The History of the Peloponnesian War*
Frederick Jackson Turner's *The Significance of the Frontier in American History*
Odd Arne Westad's *The Global Cold War: Third World Interventions And The Making Of Our Times*

The Macat Library By Discipline

LITERATURE

Chinua Achebe's *An Image of Africa: Racism in Conrad's Heart of Darkness*
Roland Barthes's *Mythologies*
Homi K. Bhabha's *The Location of Culture*
Judith Butler's *Gender Trouble*
Simone De Beauvoir's *The Second Sex*
Ferdinand De Saussure's *Course in General Linguistics*
T. S. Eliot's *The Sacred Wood: Essays on Poetry and Criticism*
Zora Neale Huston's *Characteristics of Negro Expression*
Toni Morrison's *Playing in the Dark: Whiteness in the American Literary Imagination*
Edward Said's *Orientalism*
Gayatri Chakravorty Spivak's *Can the Subaltern Speak?*
Mary Wollstonecraft's *A Vindication of the Rights of Women*
Virginia Woolf's *A Room of One's Own*

PHILOSOPHY

Elizabeth Anscombe's *Modern Moral Philosophy*
Hannah Arendt's *The Human Condition*
Aristotle's *Metaphysics*
Aristotle's *Nicomachean Ethics*
Edmund Gettier's *Is Justified True Belief Knowledge?*
Georg Wilhelm Friedrich Hegel's *Phenomenology of Spirit*
David Hume's *Dialogues Concerning Natural Religion*
David Hume's *The Enquiry for Human Understanding*
Immanuel Kant's *Religion within the Boundaries of Mere Reason*
Immanuel Kant's *Critique of Pure Reason*
Søren Kierkegaard's *The Sickness Unto Death*
Søren Kierkegaard's *Fear and Trembling*
C. S. Lewis's *The Abolition of Man*
Alasdair MacIntyre's *After Virtue*
Marcus Aurelius's *Meditations*
Friedrich Nietzsche's *On the Genealogy of Morality*
Friedrich Nietzsche's *Beyond Good and Evil*
Plato's *Republic*
Plato's *Symposium*
Jean-Jacques Rousseau's *The Social Contract*
Gilbert Ryle's *The Concept of Mind*
Baruch Spinoza's *Ethics*
Sun Tzu's *The Art of War*
Ludwig Wittgenstein's *Philosophical Investigations*

POLITICS

Benedict Anderson's *Imagined Communities*
Aristotle's *Politics*
Bernard Bailyn's *The Ideological Origins of the American Revolution*
Edmund Burke's *Reflections on the Revolution in France*
John C. Calhoun's *A Disquisition on Government*
Ha-Joon Chang's *Kicking Away the Ladder*
Hamid Dabashi's *Iran: A People Interrupted*
Hamid Dabashi's *Theology of Discontent: The Ideological Foundation of the Islamic Revolution in Iran*
Robert Dahl's *Democracy and its Critics*
Robert Dahl's *Who Governs?*
David Brion Davis's *The Problem of Slavery in the Age of Revolution*

Alexis De Tocqueville's *Democracy in America*
James Ferguson's *The Anti-Politics Machine*
Frank Dikotter's *Mao's Great Famine*
Sheila Fitzpatrick's *Everyday Stalinism*
Eric Foner's *Reconstruction: America's Unfinished Revolution, 1863-1877*
Milton Friedman's *Capitalism and Freedom*
Francis Fukuyama's *The End of History and the Last Man*
John Lewis Gaddis's *We Now Know: Rethinking Cold War History*
Ernest Gellner's *Nations and Nationalism*
David Graeber's *Debt: the First 5000 Years*
Antonio Gramsci's *The Prison Notebooks*
Alexander Hamilton, John Jay & James Madison's *The Federalist Papers*
Friedrich Hayek's *The Road to Serfdom*
Christopher Hill's *The World Turned Upside Down*
Thomas Hobbes's *Leviathan*
John A. Hobson's *Imperialism: A Study*
Samuel P. Huntington's *The Clash of Civilizations and the Remaking of World Order*
Tony Judt's *Postwar: A History of Europe Since 1945*
David C. Kang's *China Rising: Peace, Power and Order in East Asia*
Paul Kennedy's *The Rise and Fall of Great Powers*
Robert Keohane's *After Hegemony*
Martin Luther King Jr.'s *Why We Can't Wait*
Henry Kissinger's *World Order: Reflections on the Character of Nations and the Course of History*
John Locke's *Two Treatises of Government*
Niccolò Machiavelli's *The Prince*
Thomas Robert Malthus's *An Essay on the Principle of Population*
Mahmood Mamdani's *Citizen and Subject: Contemporary Africa And The Legacy Of Late Colonialism*
Karl Marx's *Capital*
John Stuart Mill's *On Liberty*
John Stuart Mill's *Utilitarianism*
Hans Morgenthau's *Politics Among Nations*
Thomas Paine's *Common Sense*
Thomas Paine's *Rights of Man*
Thomas Piketty's *Capital in the Twenty-First Century*
Robert D. Putman's *Bowling Alone*
John Rawls's *Theory of Justice*
Jean-Jacques Rousseau's *The Social Contract*
Theda Skocpol's *States and Social Revolutions*
Adam Smith's *The Wealth of Nations*
Sun Tzu's *The Art of War*
Henry David Thoreau's *Civil Disobedience*
Thucydides's *The History of the Peloponnesian War*
Kenneth Waltz's *Theory of International Politics*
Max Weber's *Politics as a Vocation*
Odd Arne Westad's *The Global Cold War: Third World Interventions And The Making Of Our Times*

POSTCOLONIAL STUDIES

Roland Barthes's *Mythologies*
Frantz Fanon's *Black Skin, White Masks*
Homi K. Bhabha's *The Location of Culture*
Gustavo Gutiérrez's *A Theology of Liberation*
Edward Said's *Orientalism*
Gayatri Chakravorty Spivak's *Can the Subaltern Speak?*

PSYCHOLOGY

Gordon Allport's *The Nature of Prejudice*
Alan Baddeley & Graham Hitch's *Aggression: A Social Learning Analysis*
Albert Bandura's *Aggression: A Social Learning Analysis*
Leon Festinger's *A Theory of Cognitive Dissonance*
Sigmund Freud's *The Interpretation of Dreams*
Betty Friedan's *The Feminine Mystique*
Michael R. Gottfredson & Travis Hirschi's *A General Theory of Crime*
Eric Hoffer's *The True Believer: Thoughts on the Nature of Mass Movements*
William James's *Principles of Psychology*
Elizabeth Loftus's *Eyewitness Testimony*
A. H. Maslow's *A Theory of Human Motivation*
Stanley Milgram's *Obedience to Authority*
Steven Pinker's *The Better Angels of Our Nature*
Oliver Sacks's *The Man Who Mistook His Wife For a Hat*
Richard Thaler & Cass Sunstein's *Nudge: Improving Decisions About Health, Wealth and Happiness*
Amos Tversky's *Judgment under Uncertainty: Heuristics and Biases*
Philip Zimbardo's *The Lucifer Effect*

SCIENCE

Rachel Carson's *Silent Spring*
William Cronon's *Nature's Metropolis: Chicago And The Great West*
Alfred W. Crosby's *The Columbian Exchange*
Charles Darwin's *On the Origin of Species*
Richard Dawkin's *The Selfish Gene*
Thomas Kuhn's *The Structure of Scientific Revolutions*
Geoffrey Parker's *Global Crisis: War, Climate Change and Catastrophe in the Seventeenth Century*
Mathis Wackernagel & William Rees's *Our Ecological Footprint*

SOCIOLOGY

Michelle Alexander's *The New Jim Crow: Mass Incarceration in the Age of Colorblindness*
Gordon Allport's *The Nature of Prejudice*
Albert Bandura's *Aggression: A Social Learning Analysis*
Hanna Batatu's *The Old Social Classes And The Revolutionary Movements Of Iraq*
Ha-Joon Chang's *Kicking Away the Ladder*
W. E. B. Du Bois's *The Souls of Black Folk*
Émile Durkheim's *On Suicide*
Frantz Fanon's *Black Skin, White Masks*
Frantz Fanon's *The Wretched of the Earth*
Eric Foner's *Reconstruction: America's Unfinished Revolution, 1863-1877*
Eugene Genovese's *Roll, Jordan, Roll: The World the Slaves Made*
Jack Goldstone's *Revolution and Rebellion in the Early Modern World*
Antonio Gramsci's *The Prison Notebooks*
Richard Herrnstein & Charles A Murray's *The Bell Curve: Intelligence and Class Structure in American Life*
Eric Hoffer's *The True Believer: Thoughts on the Nature of Mass Movements*
Jane Jacobs's *The Death and Life of Great American Cities*
Robert Lucas's *Why Doesn't Capital Flow from Rich to Poor Countries?*
Jay Macleod's *Ain't No Makin' It: Aspirations and Attainment in a Low Income Neighborhood*
Elaine May's *Homeward Bound: American Families in the Cold War Era*
Douglas McGregor's *The Human Side of Enterprise*
C. Wright Mills's *The Sociological Imagination*

Thomas Piketty's *Capital in the Twenty-First Century*
Robert D. Putman's *Bowling Alone*
David Riesman's *The Lonely Crowd: A Study of the Changing American Character*
Edward Said's *Orientalism*
Joan Wallach Scott's *Gender and the Politics of History*
Theda Skocpol's *States and Social Revolutions*
Max Weber's *The Protestant Ethic and the Spirit of Capitalism*

THEOLOGY

Augustine's *Confessions*
Benedict's *Rule of St Benedict*
Gustavo Gutiérrez's *A Theology of Liberation*
Carole Hillenbrand's *The Crusades: Islamic Perspectives*
David Hume's *Dialogues Concerning Natural Religion*
Immanuel Kant's *Religion within the Boundaries of Mere Reason*
Ernst Kantorowicz's *The King's Two Bodies: A Study in Medieval Political Theology*
Søren Kierkegaard's *The Sickness Unto Death*
C. S. Lewis's *The Abolition of Man*
Saba Mahmood's *The Politics of Piety: The Islamic Revival and the Feminist Subject*
Baruch Spinoza's *Ethics*
Keith Thomas's *Religion and the Decline of Magic*

COMING SOON

Chris Argyris's *The Individual and the Organisation*
Seyla Benhabib's *The Rights of Others*
Walter Benjamin's *The Work Of Art in the Age of Mechanical Reproduction*
John Berger's *Ways of Seeing*
Pierre Bourdieu's *Outline of a Theory of Practice*
Mary Douglas's *Purity and Danger*
Roland Dworkin's *Taking Rights Seriously*
James G. March's *Exploration and Exploitation in Organisational Learning*
Ikujiro Nonaka's *A Dynamic Theory of Organizational Knowledge Creation*
Griselda Pollock's *Vision and Difference*
Amartya Sen's *Inequality Re-Examined*
Susan Sontag's *On Photography*
Yasser Tabbaa's *The Transformation of Islamic Art*
Ludwig von Mises's *Theory of Money and Credit*

Macat Disciplines

Access the greatest ideas and thinkers across entire disciplines, including

FEMINISM, GENDER AND QUEER STUDIES

Simone De Beauvoir's
The Second Sex

Michel Foucault's
History of Sexuality

Betty Friedan's
The Feminine Mystique

Saba Mahmood's
*The Politics of Piety:
The Islamic Revival and
the Feminist Subject*

Joan Wallach Scott's
*Gender and the
Politics of History*

Mary Wollstonecraft's
*A Vindication of the
Rights of Woman*

Virginia Woolf's
A Room of One's Own

Judith Butler's
Gender Trouble

Macat analyses are available from all good bookshops and libraries.

Access hundreds of analyses through one, multimedia tool.
Join free for one month **library.macat.com**

Macat Disciplines

*Access the greatest ideas and thinkers
across entire disciplines, including*

INEQUALITY

Ha-Joon Chang's, *Kicking Away the Ladder*

David Graeber's, *Debt: The First 5000 Years*

Robert E. Lucas's, *Why Doesn't Capital Flow from
Rich To Poor Countries?*

Thomas Piketty's, *Capital in the Twenty-First Century*

Amartya Sen's, *Inequality Re-Examined*

Mahbub Ul Haq's, *Reflections on Human Development*

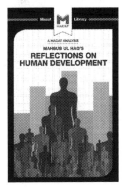

Macat analyses are available from all good bookshops and libraries.

Access hundreds of analyses through one, multimedia tool.

Join free for one month **library.macat.com**

Printed in the United States
by Baker & Taylor Publisher Services